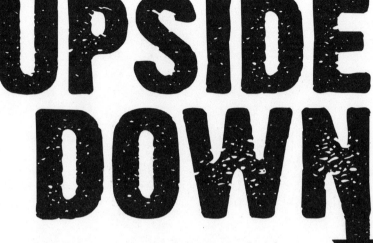

UPSIDE DOWN

Madness, Murder, and the
Perfect Marriage

UPSIDE DOWN

Madness, Murder, and the Perfect Marriage

JERID M. FISHER

PELICAN PUBLISHING COMPANY
GRETNA 2013

Library of Congress Cataloging-in-Publication Data

Fisher, Jerid M.
  Upside down : madness, murder, and the perfect marriage / by
Jerid M. Fisher.
     pages cm
  ISBN 978-1-4556-1837-8 (hardcover : alk. paper) – ISBN 978-1-
4556-1838-5 (e-book) 1. Wells, Timothy D. 2. Murder–New York
(State)–Rochester–Case studies. 3. College teachers–New York
(State)–Rochester–Case studies. I. Title.
  HV6534.R624F57 2013
  364.152'3092–dc23
                                          2013013526

Printed in the United States of America
Published by Pelican Publishing Company, Inc.
1000 Burmaster Street, Gretna, Louisiana 70053

*To my parents, Drs. Rhoda and
Seymour Fisher, who inspired me to write*

CONTENTS

ACKNOWLEDGMENTS

I am grateful for the support of so many over the years that it has taken me to write this book. My assistant, Jaime Lasda, has done a yeoman's job from the proposal to the finished manuscript. Her technical-writing skills and her tenacity have been incredible assets to this project.

I would also like to thank James Nobles, Esq., for inviting me to be his expert in this case, encouraging me to write this book, and helping secure the technical materials needed for the accurate reconstruction of the events depicted herein.

To my longtime friends and graphic-design collaborators, Paul and Janet Smith, thank you guys for your infinite creativity. A big thanks to Jen Soltys for her marketing expertise and her ongoing support. Paula and Don Bataille have provided critical insights into Tim Wells' and Christine Sevilla's life stories and for that I am deeply indebted.

To my late English teacher Kay Kasberger—wherever she is, I hope she knows how deeply she touched my life. To Dr. Richard Ciccone, thank you for your wonderful friendship and mentorship over the many years we have known each other.

Many thanks to Carrie Wells for her soul-searching candor in describing her early life with Tim. It needs to be said that I know how difficult this was for her.

To Riley as well as my dogs, Beau and Maverick—I thank my pups for their constant and unconditional love. You are our best friends.

I thank Tim Wells for his continued willingness to look within himself. There is nothing that can bring Christine back or change the terrible events of November 30, 2009, but perhaps his story will inspire another lost soul to reach out for help before it is too late.

INTRODUCTION

Shortly after Christine Sevilla's murder, Tim Wells' defense attorney asked Dr. Jerid Fisher to serve as his forensic neuropsychological expert. In this capacity, Dr. Fisher met with Wells on multiple occasions in the Monroe County jail following his arrest. Their meetings were focused on detailed interviews and formal testing that Dr. Fisher conducted to assess Wells' psychological makeup and cognitive abilities.

Dr. Fisher also spent time in the couple's home—the crime scene—sifting through many intimate facets of their lives. One year after the murder and shortly before Wells was formally sentenced and moved to a prison, Dr. Fisher and Wells agreed that this book should be written and the story be told. In the two years that followed, they regularly corresponded by letter about a range of topics that were critical to getting his side of the story right. In December 2011, Dr. Fisher made the long drive across New York state to the Clinton Correctional Facility, where he was once again able to sit privately with Wells for many hours, interviewing him further for this book.

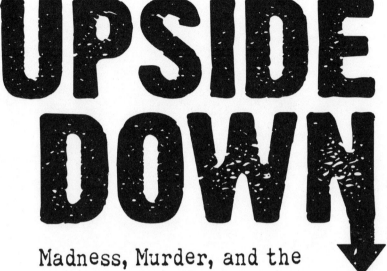

Madness, Murder, and the
Perfect Marriage

CHAPTER 1

A GENTLEMAN'S GENTLEMAN

The problem was the body lying on the floor in the mudroom.

During their nineteen years of marriage, Timothy Wells liked to say he and Christine Sevilla had never fought. They had found each other in the choir of the First Unitarian Church, and they still sang together. They were a well-educated, left-leaning, cultured couple. Tim was a professor at the Rochester Institute of Technology, and Christine was a photographer and environmental activist. Friends said you did not think of one without thinking of the other. They held hands in public. By all accounts, everyone believed that Tim and Christine had the perfect marriage. They were a symbol of genuine adoration.

What everyone didn't know was how depressed Tim had been in the fall of 2009. He was feeling more and more desperate. He was really in trouble. Logical to a fault, he said later, "In the past, there would always be some solution to a problem. I was always able to find some way to keep going—in essence, another way to keep people from thinking badly of me."

Above all, the one person he didn't want to disappoint was his wife. She had no idea how far he had fallen. Tim recalled that on this Monday morning, November 30, after the long Thanksgiving weekend, he was "desperately trying to keep things hidden" from her. He had decided that there was only one way out.

Tim and Christine lived in a white ranch house, constructed as a contemporary-style builder's model in the 1960s, on Springwood Lane, a street lined with mature trees in Pittsford, an affluent suburb of Rochester, New York. They both had failed prior marriages and were childless, but they had their twelve-year-old springer spaniel, Anna Riley (she answered to the name "Riley"). Tim even referred to the three of them as "the pack." The house received plenty of light, especially from the floor-to-ceiling windows that lined the entire back wall of the living room. Tim had been a music major in college, and often, after finishing the dinner dishes, he and Christine sat in there with Riley, singing and playing the various musical instruments they collected. This was also where Christine sat with her laptop, e-mailing friends about local environmental causes.

On the morning of November 30, 2009, Christine was doing just that, setting up a meeting by e-mail with Steven Daniel, another environmental activist. As Tim understood it, she was about to leave for the Starbucks in Pittsford. Lacking a formal office, Christine frequently held meetings at local coffee shops.

But Tim wasn't thinking too clearly that morning. He was

The couple enjoyed nearly twenty happy years at their house at 4 Springwood Lane in Pittsford, a charming suburb of Rochester, until that final November morning. (Police photo)

preoccupied with a grave problem. One decision he was clear about—he had resolved to kill himself. He couldn't stand absorbing any more failures.

At that very moment, he was supposed to be standing in front of a group of students at RIT, teaching a new course. But he couldn't bring himself to go. In the past few years, he had fallen badly behind the constant advances being made in computer science. Tim preferred death to the embarrassment of being uncloaked as a fraud.

The problem was what to do about Christine. Learning of his failures would devastate her. She was very proud of being married to a college professor. Tim had convinced himself that killing Christine would spare her from a life without him. She had told him many times, "You are the only one who would put up with me."

From the living room, Tim saw Christine preparing to leave. He knew that when she returned, the perfect world they shared would be shattered. As she put on her coat to leave, she had their cordless home phone in her hand. She often called the person she was going to meet just before she left.

At that moment he made up his mind. "This has to end," he told himself. As he related it, he calmly

Tim referred to their family as "the pack." Joined at the hip, they went everywhere together. They were known as the perfect couple for good reason—they made each other so happy. (Courtesy of Timothy D. Wells)

walked into the mudroom until he reached Christine, and he placed his hands around her throat. He recalled, "The look on her face was so startled." Though Tim wasn't strong, he was six-foot-three and Christine was a tiny five-one. He slowly lowered her to the floor. Tim could not specify the amount of time he spent in the act of killing Christine or how long he stayed by her body on the floor. All he recalled was that "it felt loving."

The perfect man, as his first wife's friends used to call him, had used strangulation, one of the most intimate, protracted means of murder, to kill his devoted wife.

The myth that Tim and Christine were the ideal suburban couple was shattered. "This shook people," Scott Tayler, co-minister at the First Unitarian Church, would tell the local paper. "The question wasn't why—it was: 'Can I trust? Can I trust life? Can I trust my own judgment?'"

This awful day of reckoning had been a long time in the making. In virtually every avenue of Tim's life, he faced mounting losses and failures that he tried to conceal from Christine. For the entire year of 2009, Tim taught six online courses to a paltry total of nineteen students. With such a low head count, paying attention to the students and their needs would seem like a simple task, but student critiques of Tim's teaching were scathing. One student protested, "I'm amazed this person still has a job. I've never imagined teaching could be so hands-off. I could have had the same experience with an online chat room. The professor added no value." Another student review was even stronger in its disdain for Professor Wells: "Worst course ever! My cat could have taught this course better."

Tim had been struggling for quite some time with depression, helplessness, and hopelessness. Among his numerous failures was his dismissal just three weeks earlier, on November 11, from a Ph.D. program in media psychology at the Fielding Institute. He was not able to satisfy even the minimum academic requirements. So far he had accrued more than $64,300 in student loans. He was so worried about preserving his perfect image with Christine that he hid this debt from her—as well as the more disturbing fact that he had been thrown out of the program. When Tim received the e-mail notification, he watched for the postman so that Christine wouldn't see the certified letter documenting his dismissal.

His entire academic career had been crashing down around him. Earlier in the year, on February 23, Tim received an e-mail from Jeffrey Lasky, head of RIT's Information Sciences and Technologies Department, stating, "It is my unpleasant task to bring you the bad news that the college has decided to suspend the Learning and Knowledge Management Systems program." Tim had created this program with great pride in late 2005. His boss made this decision because it was so unpopular.

Furthering his depression was a terrible loss in his personal life. His older sister Judy, with whom he was very close, had been diagnosed with cancer. That summer, Tim donated bone marrow to save her life. He had gone to visit her repeatedly in Ohio to provide comfort. Yet his efforts failed to make any difference. Judy had died in September.

Tim's ever-deepening downward spiral reached its nadir that November morning. Because RIT's academic calendar was structured around a trimester schedule, he was expected to start teaching two new classes that day, one at 10:00 A.M. and the other at 12:30. But at age fifty-seven, Tim had fallen seriously behind in his field. Information technology was changing and evolving rapidly. Like a tired runner falling farther behind other competitors in a long-distance race, Tim simply lacked the energy and motivation to keep up.

Tim had done practically nothing to prepare for the two new

classes. The evening before, when he should have been writing his lectures, he instead chose to join Christine in a three-hour rehearsal of their Madrigalia choral group. Singing was one of a few remaining sanctuaries for Tim. He had a beautiful singing voice, and singing in Madrigalia affirmed his worth in a way that working no longer could. Tim knew he should be preparing to teach but comforted himself by thinking, "What will be will be. I've bluffed my way before." By the time Christine and Tim returned home from choir practice, it was too late for him to prepare for his lectures.

Tim suffered from insomnia that night, as he often did. Not wishing for Christine to know about his troubled sleep, he used Riley's aging bladder as an excuse to get out of bed. Come dawn, Tim was no better. Now he was too exhausted to prepare. He fed Riley and then brought Christine coffee and toast in their bedroom around seven. Rather than use this last remaining opportunity to prepare, Tim asked Christine to go to the YMCA in Perinton, just a few minutes down the road, for a morning workout. In order to teach his first class, he should have departed for RIT by eight. Nevertheless, at eight thirty, Tim and Christine left their home for what would be their last trip to the YMCA. They swam together and Tim took a sauna, their usual exercise rituals.

They didn't return home until nearly ten. Tim glanced at his watch, imagining his students blankly staring at the classroom clock at that very moment. After he and Christine hung their coats in the closet, Christine would spend the final minutes of her life e-mailing colleagues about upcoming conservation causes. Her last message, stamped 9:55:47 A.M., offered not a hint of what was about to happen. It was a brief message to a colleague discussing an upcoming meeting about a planned canal park.

As Tim gazed out the back windows, a wave of anxiety rose from his stomach into his throat. He was clutched by an extreme tightness he had never felt before. In his soft, professorial voice, he tried to let Christine know about his doubts, telling her, "I'm nervous about these courses."

She looked up at him with an incredulous smile and reassured him, "You'll do fine. Your students love you. You can teach on personality alone."

She had a point. For the last few years Tim had always been able to come up with something: something to tell Christine, something to tell his students, something to tell himself, something to hide behind. Yet the situation had deteriorated far past anything she ever could have imagined. He always kept his feelings to himself, and he kept them from himself as well. Tim identified with Mr. Spock, of "Star Trek," a half-Vulcan, half-human character. Vulcan was a planet where the inhabitants suppressed their emotions in the pursuit of pure logic. Spock abhorred the intrusion of emotion and tried to maintain a cold and steely distance from his feelings. Strong emotions were alien to Spock, just as they were to Tim.

That's why, now that the crisis was upon him, he felt paralyzed. He thought, "This has to end. I knew this last day would come."

Tim knew how much Christine had invested in being the wife of a professor. Appearances mattered to her. She even wore dress boots to her wetlands photo shoots, just in case she ran into anyone. Tim could not imagine shattering the perfect image they cultivated in the Rochester community. "I knew I had failed," he later said. "I had failed them."

The world Tim and Christine had created together was unsustainable. A thought came to him—"the pack has to end"—and seized hold of him like a mantra.

Now he had carried out the first step of his self-imagined

Christine's bathroom vanity at 4 Springwood Lane was filled with beauty products. She never went out without looking her best. (Police photo)

death pact. Christine's body was sprawled on the gray diamond tiles of the mudroom floor.

He didn't feel any remorse, not just yet. Instead he felt an overwhelming sense of relief. He gazed around and saw Riley. Their black-and-white dog had a white stripe that ran between her eyes, making her face look like a mask. She was sitting in the kitchen, in what Tim called her cooking spot. That was where she sat and watched Tim cook, as he so often did for Christine.

Tim later wrote down what happened next.

> We walked into the living room and looked out the windows. It was beautiful. And I felt so much better. Ending all of us was such a comforting thought. It was such a relief not to be going to RIT. We were spared the disappointments of my failures. No worry about the Ph.D. program. No worries about the research projects. No worry about who will take care of Riley, or who will take care of Christine or the house. No one to disappoint or disapprove.

Tim gazed through the floor-to-ceiling windows in his living room at the sere beauty of that late-fall day. Moments later, he concluded that the pack had to die. (Police photo)

The next consideration was Riley, who stood expectantly at his side. Tim was her primary caretaker. A year before,

Riley was Tim and Christine's only "child." Tim, a proud and devoted parent, prepared a special duck dinner for her every week. (Courtesy of Timothy D. Wells)

Riley developed a strange skin condition that the vet felt would be cured with a special duck diet. Each week, Tim dutifully made a special trip to the near-by Wegmans supermarket to buy a whole duck. He would simmer the duck in a large stovetop pot with vegetables. After a year, Riley's skin condition was no better, but Tim basked in Christine's praise for his dedication to such causes. "Thank God you are here," she would say, expressing her appreciation for all the things he did.

That was all Tim had wanted, her approval. His abject submission to her desires had set the stage for a murder that, from the outside looking in, makes no sense. In the days after the terrible news came to light, people would ask, "Why didn't he just divorce her if their problems were so bad?" But Tim would never do that. He could not imagine the possibility of her living without him. Viewed through this distorted lens, Tim's characterization of Christine's murder as a mercy killing makes a perverse kind of sense.

Looking through the galley kitchen, Tim could see Christine lying motionless on the mudroom floor. Now he had to carry out the rest of his ill-conceived plan. Although he had thought about suicide before, it had never advanced beyond the vague whim of turning his car into the path of oncoming traffic. He realized the three of them—Christine, Riley, and himself—should die together. They had been a pack for so many years. Such a departure was only fitting.

He returned to the mudroom and looked down at his dead wife. That's when he noticed the phone was still lying on the floor. No sound was coming out of it. He picked it up and replaced it on its charging stand on the kitchen counter.

Tim had thought he would kill the dog and then himself right in the house, but he changed his mind. "I just thought, 'Get away.' I would take her someplace."

The more Tim considered this idea, the more convinced he became. "This wasn't the right place. This was our home." A TV miniseries he had watched recently, "Masada," came to his mind. It told the tragic story of a Roman siege that ended a Jewish rebellion in 73 C.E. The Jews committed mass suicide rather than surrender to the invading Romans. Tim thought, "They had no choice. They were under siege. But we have time now. Maybe we'll go to Horizon Hill." Even at this horrific moment, Tim sought sanctuary in his thoughts by reflecting on a series he had seen.

Horizon Hill was an area of wooded hiking trails barely a mile and a half from their home. The top of the hill provided panoramic views of the city of Rochester. That was one reason why he and Christine liked to hike it. Ending the three of them there, he thought, would please her.

The plan for a final rite was forming. "I began to think about the end. We could spread a blanket. We could be somewhere we enjoyed going to and have a glass of wine." Out in the sere beauty of late autumn, he would kill Riley, and then he would kill himself—a humane ending, like in "Masada."

Tim spent the next thirty minutes walking around their home. He haphazardly tidied things up for the last time, just as Christine would have wanted. With the end near, he was in a reflective mood. Tim glanced at the cookbooks lined up on the shelf in the tiny galley kitchen, then up at the skylights. At this moment, he knew he would never see any of this again. Tim continued to walk around the house, Riley trailing faithfully behind. All the while, as if in a dream, Tim reminded himself, "This is the last time I will be here."

He was free. He later wrote in his diary: "Thought about not teaching, not trying to work on Ph.D., not trying to make progress on research. It feels wonderful! If it weren't for the tragic situation, I would be giddy."

The living room would be the hardest to leave, always the central gathering place for Tim, Christine, and Riley. The ceiling was lined with dark-stained exposed beams. At one end stood a profusion of musical instruments arranged on stands. A pair of bongo drums flanked a banjo and acoustic guitar. An electric piano, bass guitar, another acoustic guitar, and instrument cases faced them. Imposing speakers were mounted atop the long bookcases lining the wall opposite

Lifelong music lovers, Tim and Christine filled their living room with the various instruments they played. (Courtesy of Timothy D. Wells)

the windows. At the far end, above a small wood-burning fireplace, were arrayed a half-dozen of Christine's nature photographs, strikingly framed with broad white mattes.

Although he meant to tidy up, Tim didn't accomplish too much in his dazed state. One of his household duties was to make their bed. Today, he merely pulled the covers up over the pillows. Tim overlooked several days' worth of newspapers stacked on the dining-room table. Nor did he touch any of Christine's things, such as her cardboard portfolio case also lying on the table, or the shelf in the kitchen where she sorted through their mail and planned activities and meetings. Prominent among the scattered papers was literature from Lumin Guild, the name of Christine's information technology company. Its letterhead grandly proclaimed that it designed instructional programs and solutions. In reality, Lumin Guild was a moribund concern that had cost Tim at least ten thousand dollars in each of the previous two years.

Now it was time to leave all of this behind. Despite being so tall, Tim was weak. In order to move Christine, he ended up holding her under her arms and walking backward, dragging her heels on the floor. He recalled, "I did position her in a comfortable position. But getting her to the car was not elegant." He struggled with Christine's dead weight as he pulled her through the doorway toward the two-car garage. The ranch house was connected to the garage by a short breezeway. In one corner was tucked a little doggie bed for Riley. Out back was a cement patio, its table and chairs sitting forlornly in the chill of late November.

Through the next doorway, he entered the unfinished garage, lined with gardening tools and a metal rack that held supplies for numerous home improvements. A four-door gray Saab with the license plate LUMIN was closest to him.

Tim's four-door steel-blue Saturn was parked on the far side. Beyond his Saturn was an open doorway leading into a spare room that at one time had served as a studio for Christine's photographs and paintings. In recent years, it had been used only as storage space for extra furniture, outdated computer equipment from Lumin Guild, and the like, symbolic of the company's fading viability.

Tim did not take long to decide between the Saab and the Saturn. He always took the Saturn, and that's the car Riley rode in too, because Tim had laid out a tan blanket in the backseat. Riley was coming along for this final ride. It was necessary for the pack to end together.

Tim deposited Christine's lifeless body in the front passenger seat, then realized the problem this would pose. "I didn't want anybody to see anything," he said later. Christine would have to ride along in the trunk, where she would be out of sight. But Tim knew he could not leave her in the trunk in plain view. What if he needed to open the trunk at some point? "The trunk was big and empty. I needed something to fold around Christine. I'd also need something to use as a sled to get her up the hill. I knew I couldn't carry her up to the overlook at Horizon Hill. The tarp was there next to the car. I used it to haul leaves up the back hill to the curb." After placing the tarp in the trunk, he struggled to place his wife's dead body atop it, then folded it over her, hiding her from prying eyes.

Returning to the house, Tim collected Christine's purse, then his from the top kitchen shelf. He had long ago abandoned concern of maintaining a masculine image. Without any qualms, he had carried a purse for years. Tim frequently referred to himself proudly as a "gentleman's gentleman." Despite his handsome looks and tall frame, he could never be described as macho. In no way did he look like a man who would strangle his wife with his bare hands.

While he was a full-fledged heterosexual, he and Christine had not had sex for the last five years. This may have been because his testosterone level was so low. In fact, his primary-care physician had prescribed a testosterone supplement, but Tim never filled it. He believed that increasing his testosterone levels would lower his threshold for brutish behaviors, which would be in stark contrast to the image he had cultivated of being a gentleman's gentleman.

Tim then gathered up a dirty sheet lying on the mudroom floor. The ground in upstate New York is frozen in late November, and he would need this buffer to insulate their bodies from the cold earth, once he found their final resting place. He would position Christine on it before killing Riley and himself.

The pack had to end. But Tim had not yet decided how he would kill the dog and himself. "Masada" again popped into his mind. At the end, the Jews had committed mass suicide by "humane" knife wounds rather than surrender. This was the way they would go, he decided. "In the movies the leaders at Masada went to the butcher and asked how he kept kosher—killing the animals without pain. They cut their throats. I couldn't see how I could do that to myself, but I would kill Riley that way. I would cut down the length of my arms." Tim grabbed a long filet knife from a kitchen drawer.

He also took a corkscrew and two bottles of wine. "I didn't know if I'd want red or white," he recalled, so he grabbed one of each. Tim would be "civilized" to the end, toasting to the pack's demise. He had developed quite the taste for the grape in the past few years, drinking three or four glasses a night to numb his blue moods. Grabbing Riley's leash, he put the purses in the front of the car and the wine, leash, and knife behind the driver's seat. Without much thought, he threw the corkscrew into a paper bag. He opened the main garage door to the driveway. Riley went out and peed, then trotted back and jumped in the backseat. Tim placed the sheet in the trunk, closed it, backed the car out, and closed the garage door.

In some ways, the trip seemed like just another family outing. He and Christine had made car trips with Riley so many times before. Riley was standing up, leaning her behind against the backseat cushion, her paws braced for the turns the car would make during Tim's journey. She wagged her tail, oblivious to the plans Tim had for her. As Tim mentally clicked through his usual departure checklist, the finality of this last trip together set in. Under other circumstances, he might have gone back in to be sure the patio door was locked, but now this did not matter.

Tim couldn't help but notice that the seat next to him was vacant. It would never be filled by Christine again. Her energy, her impish smiles, her need for him, had all been extinguished. Now she was lying in the trunk. No one would know how shamefully Tim had betrayed his wife's trust in their perfect marriage, at least not until he was already past the point of caring what people thought of him.

"I looked at the house with sadness. It didn't look like much from the front. It was perfect for us. We had done so much here. We were so comfortable. I loved being here with Riley and Christine, away from the world. In recent years, Christine would say how she hated leaving our home—she said she was becoming a homebody. I could never wait to get home from RIT. Christine often encouraged me to blow off office hours so we could eat lunch together and go to a park to take pictures and walk Riley. We planned to redesign the entrance when we replaced the driveway—someday, soon. But that didn't matter. We won't be back."

Their shared life of nineteen years was now over. The perfect marriage would now be matched by the perfect ending. All he had to do was find the perfect spot to lay them all out.

CHAPTER 2

PLACES I REMEMBER

His thoughts unfocused, Tim drove a mile and a half down the road. "Horizon Hill was the park I had in mind," he said later. "Most of our walks with Riley were there." Through this wooded area runs a rugged stretch of the thirteen-mile Crescent Trail. Christine was an active member of the Crescent Trail Association, which later would memorialize her as a tireless advocate for the protection of plants and natural habitat.

Although Tim had picked this as the perfect final resting spot, he immediately saw the obstacles to carrying out his plan. "As we pulled up, I saw several cars in the lot. I smiled at the thought of seeing familiar faces. We knew all the regulars—not by name, but we knew all the dogs. I wondered if I'd be able to pull Christine up to the overlook." The only way to reach Horizon Hill's scenic overlook, 825 feet high, is to walk the dirt footpaths heading up the wooded glacial summit, thick with oak and hickory trees. More than the ascent, though, Tim feared encountering any of the numerous local dog walkers he knew. "A sad feeling came over me as I realized they wouldn't understand. I'd always been the nice guy. It was important that people like me. I'd always done what people expected. Now they will hate me." That decided the matter. "This wasn't the right place. There are other places."

So he set off on his macabre daylong odyssey of finding the best spot to kill himself. He turned the radio on, like always, and listened to the news. He and Christine usually listened to National Public Radio's "Morning Edition." With his springer spaniel perched restlessly in the backseat,

this outing was much like any other—with some important
exceptions. For one, his wife's dead body was lying folded in
a tarp in the trunk. Another was the fact that he should have
been teaching his classes. He had expected that RIT would
call him even before he left the house. Someone from his ten-
o'clock class must have gone down to the department office
to check on him by now. His worry about that conflicted with
his feeling of freedom from responsibility. He kept telling
himself that he was past all that now.

He headed for Lehigh Crossing Park, located in the nearby
town of Victor, just south of the New York State Thruway. The
temperature was mild for the last day in November, in the upper
thirties. Among the trails running through the park, he chose
the one that followed the bed of an old railroad that, from 1903
to 1930, traveled from Rochester southeast to Geneva, near the
head of one of central New York's Finger Lakes. Its flat grade
was easy on an older dog. As Tim walked along, he recalled
Christine capturing some beautiful images there.

Her approach to environmentalism had always been
hands on. In the best tradition of grassroots activism, she did
not try to change the world, but only her small corner of
it. She showed up when the county parks commission held
meetings. Time and time again, she argued that the local
parks should not be "improved" but left in their natural
state. An e-mail she had sent to an editor of the *Rochester City
News* that very morning showed her astute grasp of how the
powers-that-be operated:

> Attendees of the Greece Canal Park meeting on Tuesday
> night were told about the two million dollars available for
> park development, and to just brainstorm about "what
> you think we should do with the park." Some people said
> let's do nothing, don't waste money needlessly. At least do
> nothing harmful, like bisecting the park with a road. But the
> meeting discussion was focused on "how should we spend

this money?" The idea of parks as places set aside, protected and unspoiled, is an unwelcome part of the discussion when money is available for development.

That tireless voice for open spaces had been lost. In silence, Tim and Riley strolled down the old cinder railroad bed, which was often intruded upon by trees and underbrush. The two were familiar companions, but the walk wasn't the same without Christine, the third member of the pack. Christine was locked away in the Saturn's trunk, the car parked with seeming innocence in the lot near the trail. Tim did not walk more than a hundred yards before turning around and coming back.

Already Tim's focus was changing. He was not looking for a spot for the final ritual so much as "taking inventory," he said later. He wanted to visit all the places that had significance for Christine. Tim didn't remember specific thoughts, but he recalled going some places and saying, "It's nice to be here but this isn't it."

In a bizarre farewell tour, he visited many familiar spots through the day. "A memory would come to mind and we'd drive there. At each place I'd let Riley out, grab the leash, and we'd walk. It felt pleasant and nostalgic. I could remember images from Christine's shows that were taken here and there. I remembered how it felt at different times of the year."

When man and dog returned to the car at Lehigh Crossing Park, Tim decided to head over to nearby Fishers Park, a small park with picnic tables overlooking a pretty area by a stream. The bridge over the stream leads to several trails that branch off. One trail heads up over a hill to a wooded wetland and a scenic meadow beyond that. It's nice for dog walks, but that morning Tim and Riley didn't start up the hill. Tim knew this site was in no way suitable for the grand finale he had planned.

The next stop on the tour was Mendon Ponds County Park. With 2,500 acres of woodlands, ponds, wetlands, and glacially created landforms, this park was named to the National Registry of Natural Landmarks in 1969. More important to Tim, it was located near their home, and Christine had taken hundreds upon hundreds of pictures there. She had particularly loved a tiny pond known as the Devil's Bathtub. "We used to walk there so often," he later recalled.

Above all else, Christine had an affinity for wetlands. She constantly visited local marshes and swamps, taking striking photographs, often of individual flowers or other distinctive plants within them. She wrote two catalogs for photography shows about wetlands, calling them "haunting, beckoning." In her catalog for Watershed, a collection of over one hundred images of western New York wetlands, she wrote, "These places form a transitional bridge between waterway and land. I am like them

Christine was a dedicated photojournalist of wetlands in central New York. (From *Democrat and Chronicle*, April 5, 2011, © 2011 Gannett, www.democratandchronicle.com. All rights reserved. Used by permission and protected by the Copyright Laws of the United States. The printing, copying, redistribution, or retransmission of this Content without express written permission is prohibited.)

—melding boundaries, filtering all, mediating the deluge, in flux, ignored. We have a bond, wetlands and me. They share their atmosphere with me, and I honor this bond by sharing their allure through images."

The Devil's Bathtub is known as a kettle hole, a shallow body of water formed by retreating glaciers, nestled in a deep ravine. Around it rises a steep esker, a long, winding ridge of post-glacial gravel. To reach it, Tim parked in a small lot just off Pond Road, which bisects the park east to west. Next to the lot was an open-air wooden pavilion that sheltered several picnic tables. To the right lay Deep Pond, the Bathtub's larger neighbor on the other side of the ridge. Up the hill was a small meadow where Christine often found beautiful wildflowers to photograph.

Marked by a small wooden sign pointing toward the Devil's Bathtub, a narrow dirt trail led uphill, flanked by woods and overgrown decaying grass. At the top was a second picnic pavilion, overlooking the Devil's Bathtub. That area seemed to Tim like an ideal spot for the final slayings.

This would have been a poignant choice for a final resting place, as was later revealed by Steven Daniel, an environmentalist who often worked side by side with Christine. He remembered walking with her near the Devil's Bathtub once in the early fall. Christine told Steven that she would like to be cremated and have her ashes spread in the pond. He did not think much of her remark at the time, chalking it up to romanticism.

Tim's thoughts on the matter were more concrete. Helping to sharpen his focus was a small scare once they returned to the parking lot. As they came back down the hill, Riley ran ahead and greeted a young man standing by the car. The stranger, of course, had no idea what was inside the locked trunk. He gave Riley a pat on the head, then moved on to his van and drove away.

Tim was not yet convinced he had found the best spot. On they meandered toward their next destination, and possible sacrifice site, Powder Mills Park. Located close to their home, in Pittsford, the park features 380 acres and a variety of hiking trails that wind among its steep wooded hills. Tim and Christine used to walk on only two, the Daffodil and Hatchery trails. He parked at the Fish Hatchery and crossed a field toward a wetlands area. Yet he and Riley went only about a hundred yards before turning around. The impression that the Devil's Bathtub had made on him continued to linger in his mind. That really may be best.

By mid-afternoon, Tim was getting hungry. During his hazy, meandering voyage, he found himself in Brockport, twenty miles west of Rochester and home to one of the larger state universities. He pulled into a McDonald's and received another shock. "A sheriff's car was parked next to us. I followed the officers in and ordered a hamburger, coffee, and fries." Tim wasn't one to give away his secrets, though, and after the initial surprise he tuned them out. He would write:

> In later hours and days, investigators and psychologists would ask if I thought about turning myself in. No. I had not thought of it. I didn't feel guilty. I was calm, content, almost happy. Thinking back, it was more like relief. Investigators and psychologists would ask how I dealt with the weight of what I had done. I felt no weight. Ending the pack was so obvious. It wasn't a crime. I knew people wouldn't understand, but I was comfortable with what I was doing.

Tim returned to the car with his lunch, feeding Riley some of his hamburger. The journey continued. On another whim, he decided to head a long way this time, more than forty miles south to the High Tor wilderness area. This giant tract includes 1,700 acres of marsh, fed by three streams that flow into the southern end of Canandaigua Lake, one of the eleven Finger Lakes in central New York. Tim actually didn't know the name of the area, because Christine was usually the one who drove there, but he knew "it was the type of place where you expect to see a pterodactyl flying or see a dinosaur running."

By this time, the sun was declining to the west, and Tim was reminded of the duties he must perform come nightfall. Around four o'clock, he stopped at a drugstore in Naples, a tiny village southwest of Canandaigua Lake. The store had a school-supply section, and he bought a writing pad. "I needed to write a note," he thought. "Friends and family soon would know how I had failed. I couldn't hide that anymore. But they would still love Christine and Riley. That was important."

"Today I Freed Myself"

In his car in the drugstore parking lot, Tim proceeded to compose the following suicide note.

> Today I freed myself in a terrible way. I killed the ones I loved because I was a failure.
>
> Every year brings new technology that I cannot master. Every year I study media psychology that leaves me more confused.
>
> This morning I was to face another class of students and try to convince them I am an expert. I am not.
>
> I could not go to RIT again.
>
> I could not stay home.
>
> When death presented itself—I accepted.
>
> Call my brother James in Santa Barbara
>
> Call Christine's brothers—
>
> Charles Sevilla in San Diego
>
> Michael Sevilla in Lake Orion, Michigan
>
> Ask them to use what assets we have to help my sister care for my parents in Croton, Ohio
>
> Remember me with hatred
>
> Remember Christine and Riley with love
>
> > Timothy Wells

With the note written, his thoughts turned to the melancholy rites he would have to perform. That called for a drink. "I decided I would have the merlot at the end. I opened the bottle of white and poured some into the empty coffee cup." He laid the pad of paper on the front passenger seat, and there it remained until a police flashlight discovered it in the early hours of the next day.

Tim headed off, feeling better now that his suicide note was written. He felt free of the anxieties that had beset him. "My experience was not anger. It was not desperation. It felt amazing. It was not a bad feeling."

North was the next direction of this bizarre tour. Instead of High Tor, the destination was now the town of Webster, located on Irondequoit Bay, a narrow southern extension of Lake Ontario. Of interest to Tim was the wetlands section of Ellison Park, feeding into the head of the bay. Ellison was one of the parks where mountain biking was a big issue, and Christine had been vocal in her opposition of this use of the park. It was getting dark by the time Tim stopped to get gas at a Hess station on nearby Empire Boulevard. One pump was covered with a plastic bag, so he stopped alongside the one that worked. He stuck a twenty-dollar bill out the window, directing the gas-station attendant to fill his Saturn's tank.

The long drive was wearing on Riley. While she appreciated so many doggie walks, she did not like riding around so much. Riley was in a snit. "She gets that way on long drives— like our trips down to Ohio. She curls up in a light sleep. I'd stop somewhere and she'd lift her head in anticipation. I'd say, 'We're not there yet.' She'd give me an irritated sigh, put her head down, and glance up with a pathetic look—'poor me, poor me.'"

By this time Tim had returned to the Rochester metro area, only a few miles north of Springwood Lane. Yet he had made up his mind that he would never return, and he drove past it on his way to visit Mendon Ponds County Park for a second time. Now that he had stopped at so many places that he and Christine had cherished, his feelings about their final resting place had become more definite.

"The sun was close to setting when we visited Mendon Ponds again. We parked in the lower lot of the Devil's Bathtub. The road to the upper lot was closed off. We walked down past the kettle hole almost to the Kennedy bog. The light was shifting quickly—there was now more shadow than light. We walked back—up the esker—past a bench that overlooked the pond." Set down a couple of steps by itself, it faced Deep Pond. "It felt so familiar. Of course. Christine loved this area. This was the place to end."

That couldn't happen just yet, though. Even with the approach of darkness, people were taking advantage of the late-fall temperatures, especially because snow was predicted after midnight. "We heard a man on the path below calling his dog. People were still here. There would be park personnel around for hours. They probably make rounds to discourage late-night lovers and parties. All would be quiet by one or two o'clock."

He had a logistical problem as well. As the road to the upper parking lot was closed, he had to figure out a way to transport Christine's body up the hill. He couldn't possibly carry her body that far. As he returned to the lower parking lot, he saw a post deliberately blocking off vehicle access to the hiking trail—but also something that was vital to his plans. "I noticed the post near the lower shelter was removable. I could drive up to the upper shelter." He was very pleased. Everything was set for their final rites. "This was perfect."

With nighttime fallen, any further trips to the local parks would be useless, and with people and personnel still around Mendon Ponds, he could not yet carry out his plans. Tim decided to spend the evening visiting places that had held meaning for him and Christine. "Hours and days later, investigators and psychologists asked if I ever thought of running—leaving the area. The prosecutor suggested I was just looking for a place to dump the body. I had no such thought. This was not my experience. It never entered my mind. I was not running from a crime. I had simply decided we had to end." He had decided on the right place. Now he just needed the right time.

He headed back to the city of Rochester for a farewell tour of all the places that reminded him of Christine. It was a beautiful night, crisp and bright. Lights glowed with unusual definition. Passing from the suburbs into the urban area, he drove by Strong Memorial Hospital, part of the University of Rochester's medical complex. When Tim met Christine, she had been employed there as an administrator, managing outpatient clinics as well as developing staff training. He remembered how miserable Christine felt working there and how happy she was when she quit to do her own work.

Tim continued on to downtown Rochester, taking in the familiar sights. He drove through Village Gate Square, a thriving metropolitan area east of the central business district filled with restaurants and art galleries. He passed Writers & Books, one of the foremost community literary centers in the country, offering writing and poetry classes, workshops, and readings by famous visiting authors. Christine had once been invited to host a photography show there, and to add to the authenticity she used their old-fashioned metal printing press to produce some prints. Down the block, Tim also passed the studio of an artist, Steve Carpenter, where Christine had done a lot of work.

From there he wended his way out of the city back to the neighboring town of Webster. He wanted to visit the Harmony House, a former grange hall built in 1899 near Lake Ontario. These days, the Harmony House is owned by the Chorus of the Genesee, a member of the nationwide Barbershop Harmony Society. They regularly hosted singing groups, and Tim and

Christine had recently appeared there to perform duets. "I would never have had the drive to organize the concert we performed there several months ago," Tim recalled wistfully. "The topsy-turvy photo used in the newspaper [as publicity] was part of the press release she created for the concert. It was so much fun—but something I would never have done without her. She did so much. I love what she does."

Their success there reminded him of another place where they had sung so much together: the First Unitarian Church of Rochester. He drove back into the city until the church appeared behind the streetlights. The church's structure is uniquely modern, an impressive work designed by world-renowned architect Louis Kahn. Rather than the usual image of a church with a white steeple, it features a plain brick front with vertical inserts. That is because Kahn arranged the community rooms around the church, which forms the heart of the sprawling building. Its sanctuary is strikingly bold, with walls of patterned gray stones and a choir loft at the rear jutting out above the heads of the congregation. For so many years, Tim and Christine had raised their voices here to inspire their fellow parishioners to worship.

These people were stunned most of all as the word about what happened began to spread the next day. They all had marveled at how perfect Tim and Christine's match had seemed. Several of them commented later to the *Rochester Democrat and Chronicle* about how the timid professor's murder of his wife was so out of character. "He seemed to me to be not just quiet but very contained," said Nora Bredes, who had met the couple more than a decade earlier. "I felt that he was the anchor that allowed her to grow like that. He was a very solid citizen. He always knew what he did well," added Abby Chodoff, a longtime church member and close friend of Christine's. "He was willing to accompany her in whatever she wanted to try." Fellow choir member Grace Carswell noted, "They were warm with each other and looked into each other's eyes with that glance that couples exchange when there is intimacy there."

Co-minister Scott Tayler summed up the widespread shock that spread among the congregation. "The fact they were known as Tim and Christine spoke to what everyone experienced as genuine adoration. Nobody had ever seen that adoring quality as anything but precious and healthy. They were members for over fifteen years, . . . first separately and then as a couple. What brought them together, what made people proud of them, was the music program. The choir is its own community, a family, and so the fact that they fell in love there too, some of the choir people take a special participation in that. You know, two of our own fell in love here, and they felt very close not only to Tim and Christine but to the marriage of Tim and Christine."

Saddened by what he knew would be the loss of all those friends, Tim headed for the final destination of his evening rounds. South of the city was the Rochester Institute of Technology, the place where he had taught for so long. RIT is a large university, with over eighteen hundred students and nearly 250 buildings. In his old, nondescript Saturn, Tim drove through the different streets of the campus. Yet these memories brought him no joy. This was where he had experienced so many failures. His description of the school on that farewell drive would be brief and grim: "It still looked like a prison—even more so at night."

By this point, it was very late. Tim couldn't return to Mendon Ponds yet, though, because he couldn't be sure that the police had made their final rounds. Instead, he decided to head out on the highway. He'd finish his bottle of white wine. He would need all the fortification he could get to carry out his own final rites.

CHAPTER 3

A HAUNTED CRY FOR HELP

The witching hour was drawing nigh. With only hours remaining before the ceremony would begin, when he could be positive that Mendon Ponds County Park was empty, Tim headed off for a final tour of the late-fall landscape to savor his dwindling hours of life. Now that the time to carry out the rest of the plan was close, he could finally reach for some courage. "Along the road I stopped and poured more wine into the McDonald's cup. I drove an hour or so south on 390—pulled off—poured another cup of wine—drove an hour back." He took an exit south of the thruway for the road that led to Mendon Ponds. In the dark countryside, everything looked foreign, and he only remembered later that he "stopped at some dark warehouse-looking place with a dumpster" to throw out the bottle of white wine.

He drove to the lower parking lot of the Devil's Bathtub. He pulled up to the dirt path along Deep Pond. Following the plan he had devised that afternoon, he got out to remove the post. As he drove the car forward a ways, he stopped to replace the post behind him. Riley took advantage of the open car door to jump out and pee. With the post put back in place, Tim believed that no one would find them until morning. After he went a short distance on the path, his headlights illuminated an open grassy slope up to the picnic pavilion. He took a left off the path and started to drive up the hill itself. About a third of the way up, though, the tires lost traction. With his usual mechanical mindset, he decided to back down in reverse in order to realign the car for a straight shot up the incline. He started up again, trying to maintain traction. He crossed the grassy area to a thickly wooded part of the slope where the path created a gap. Yet he managed to travel only about half-way up the hill before the car began slipping out of control.

This would have to be good enough, he decided. Through the gap in the woods, he could see that the pavilion was only another hundred yards up the slope. He set the handbrake and got out.

He later recounted, "This would be fine. It was so obvious. We would spread the sheet. I'd call Riley over. She would move into me as I squatted down—she always does. She'd turn and sit and look up at me. I'd cut her throat quickly. I'd bring Christine up to the sheet and put Riley next to her. I'd have a glass of wine and cut down my arms. It was gentle and painless and clear."

He and Riley walked up the hill together and found the wooden bench where the grim ceremony would be held. The sky had not yet become overcast, although the weather was quickly changing. The ethereal quality of the lighting added to the hallowed feeling he had about the upcoming occasion. "The moon was almost full. It was beautiful and felt so right. The moon cast intricate shadows. Clouds often moved over its face setting the forest in motion. The place was alive. We walked along the esker and down the hill to the kettle hole. The sky cast moonlight across the surface of the water." Marring the idyllic reverie was a pratfall the increasingly inebriated professor had on the slick grass. "I slipped on the lower slope and broke the Styrofoam cup. I discarded the pieces, thinking, 'Some environmentalist I am.'"

At last they walked up the stairs to the pavilion. Riley sniffed around the area, and then they returned to the car. Tim opened the trunk and collected the sheet he had placed there that morning. From inside the car he scooped up the remaining bottle of wine—a Charles Shaw merlot—and the paper bag containing the corkscrew. Yet Tim's dreamy mood was suddenly replaced by alarm. The filet knife wasn't where he'd left it behind the driver's seat. With a growing panic, he looked under the seats and then all around the passenger compartment. Wondering if he had somehow remembered wrong, he went back to the trunk and checked all around the edges. He knew he hadn't placed it under Christine's body, but he couldn't find it. This puzzled him. This wasn't right. He began to feel anxious and confused. He knew he carried the knife from the kitchen.

Timothy Wells' plan of a perfect ritual ending was falling apart, much like all of the failures that had preceded it. "Investigators and psychologists would ask why I didn't just leave and get another knife," he later recalled. "It never occurred to me. It never came to mind."

Feeling unhinged, he put Riley on her leash. The plan he had been envisioning all day long was going off the rails. Nevertheless, he decided to keep on going. He could figure out the final details later.

He took the sheet, the wine bottle, and bag with the corkscrew back up the hill to the bench. He took the leash off Riley. With a heavy heart, he placed the sheet on the bench. He spread it out all along its length to put Christine and Riley on it. After opening the bottle and dropping the corkscrew back in the bag, he tried to puzzle his way forward. It was time to kill Riley. She was supposed to be killed with a cut throat like in "Masada." Then Tim would bring up Christine, drink some wine, and cut his arms. That was what was supposed to happen. That is what felt right all day. But he didn't have the knife.

The answer to the next step in the plan was lying right at hand. "Riley was the next to die. A log or a rock? There was a sharp rock near my feet. I picked it up and called Riley. She came close and I brought the rock down on her head. She fell."

Unexpectedly, he felt a sharp pain. The tip of his fourth finger—which absorbed the blow to Riley's head—stung from the impact. It was throbbing in the cold night air. And then, with the pain, came a stark reminder of what he was really doing.

Riley had been stunned, and a large splotch of blood quickly appeared on her white fur. "It was so horrible—so cruel. I felt like yelling, loudly, uncontrollably, but I don't know if I was making a sound. It felt so wrong. It was violent and primitive. I hit her two or three more times rapidly. I felt the cold tears all over my face."

Riley slumped to the ground, with another pool of blood dampening the white fur of her upper snout. He was convinced he had killed her. "She is dead. But I am shaking and crying. We have to end, but this isn't right. This was cruel and brutal."

Tim walked away, shaken by his horrible deed. Now he felt too weak to drag Christine up the hill. Nor would he be able to slide her up, not with the slope so muddy. He wrote later:

> Now I was to bring Christine up to the bench. I walked to the slope and looked down at the car. I heard my own cries now. It was supposed to be beautiful. It had all been so obvious. I couldn't bring Christine up here. I didn't think I could even walk down to the car. I didn't have the knife. How could I kill myself?

He had left behind, by the bench where he had struck Riley, the bottle of merlot plus the bag containing the corkscrew. He had drunk a lot of wine by this time. Overcome by all that had happened that day, Tim stumbled about the pavilion area until he dropped to his knees in the middle of the parking lot. He recalled, "I wanted to call for help." The display on his cell phone was dark, but he activated it. In another few moments, he punched in 911.

The dispatcher said, "This is 911." That was the start of an eighteen-minute call in which Tim became almost completely incoherent because he couldn't stop sobbing.

There was a long pause, and the dispatcher had to repeat herself. "This is 911."

Finally, sounding very confused, he replied. "Yes, this is Tim Wells. I need help."

After she asked about his present location, Tim was able to tell her he was in Mendon Ponds County Park, near the Devil's Bathtub.

"What's going on there?"

Tim couldn't answer. "I . . . uh, I . . . " He started gulping for breath, holding back a wave of tears. "I . . . I'm sorry."

"Do you need an ambulance?"

"I need an ambulance."

"What happened?"

"I . . . I ki—" Tim was breathing so hard, gasping in and out, that he couldn't form the words, nor did he want to.

"Is an officer there with you?"

"Uh, no . . . no one's here with me."

"Can you tell me what's going on?"

Tim's crying was growing worse. "I . . . I . . . I killed . . . I killed my wife."

"Okay, sir, where is she right now?"

"She's in the car, down the hill."

"Okay, can you tell me what happened?"

Tim was having a hard time getting the words out. "It was . . . ah . . . I wanted to bring her here because she loved this place."

"Okay, where exactly are you in the park right now?"

"Uh . . . there's a parking lot for the Devil's Bathtub." He was weeping so much, he couldn't say any more.

"Okay, just stay on the line with me, okay?" She asked again where he was, and he was able to give her a description of the Devil's Bathtub.

"Where is the car where she's in?"

"I pulled it up . . . near the pond."

"Near the pond? What happened? What did you do?"

At this point, Tim broke down completely, crying so loudly

that on the recording he sounds as if he were choking.

"Try and take a deep breath for me," the dispatcher said patiently. "Are you okay? Are there any weapons involved?"

"No," Tim managed to say. "There are no weapons, no."

"How did you hurt her?" Tim couldn't respond, he was sobbing so hard. "Could you tell me how you hurt her?" she persisted.

Tim still couldn't manage to speak.

"Did you drown her in the pond?"

"Ah . . . no . . . I brought her here because she loved this . . ." He broke down again in total despair.

The dispatcher, while patient with Tim's crying, needed to know vital information. "Okay, take a deep breath now. Do you know what happened? Is the car there? Are you just standing there, or where are you?"

"I'm in the parking lot, and the car is down the hill," he managed to say.

"You have to tell me what happened, okay?"

Tim had lost all control, and for another half-minute the phone was filled with his breathy sobs. "She's dead . . . a knife . . . ," he finally said.

"Where is the knife now?"

He continued crying, and she had to ask him again about the knife. "No, there is no knife," he replied.

"Where is the knife you stabbed her with?" she persisted.

"No, I didn't stab her."

"Oh, you didn't? What happened to her?"

Tim broke down again, unable to admit what he'd done. All he could say was, "I'm . . . I'm so sorry."

The dispatcher kept trying to calm him, but he was awash in drunken misery. Amid his choking gasps, he cried, "I don't know what to do!"

The dispatcher let him bawl, but when the phone went silent, she asked, "Are you still with me, Tim?"

The loud sobs broke out anew. He had lost all control, managing only to moan unintelligible sounds.

The dispatcher tried another tack. She needed him to calm down enough to tell her what the situation was, so that she could brief the officers arriving on the scene as to what sort of danger they might encounter. "Can you tell me what kind of car you have?"

Tim was so far gone, he couldn't even manage that. "A Saturn . . . ," he said at last.

"Can you tell me how old you are? Do you know when your birthday is?"

"I'm . . . fifty- . . . seven . . . 19 . . . 52 . . . "

The phone was filled with his hyperventilating for long seconds, and the dispatcher tried again. "Can you tell me what happened, Tim?"

Tim tried again, stammering, "I . . . " several times, but he couldn't say the awful word "strangle." He couldn't admit, "I strangled Christine."

For the next few minutes, Tim continued to sob uncontrollably, trying to provide the bits of information he could at the dispatcher's prodding. She managed to determine that he hadn't killed his wife in the park but had brought her there. That alone significantly reduced the threat level to the responding officers. She dug out of him that he lived in Pittsford, at 4 Springwood Lane. As he continued to cry, a police siren began to wail in the background. The first units were arriving on the scene, although they still had no idea where he was. Once the four police cars reached the lower parking lot, they spent many long minutes trying to locate him on the hill.

All the while Tim cried uncontrollably, and now that the dispatcher knew the officers were nearby, she let him grieve. Every once in a while she would ask a question, but he was crying so hard, his answers were lost amid his wracking sobs. All the initial euphoria he felt at being free of his failures had vanished. Left behind was a lonely old man whose heart was irretrievably broken. He had killed his wife. She had meant everything to him.

Finally, the 911 operator could hear the voices of police officers. They found Tim Wells kneeling on the cold pavement, crying his heart out for the awful crimes he had committed.

"Investigators and psychologists would ask why I turned myself in," Tim said later. "I was calling for help. I was calling for an end. This wasn't a crime. The thought of turning myself in was never part of my experience. I felt so confused. I couldn't find the moon."

"Do you hear the officers?" the dispatcher asked.

"Yes." Wiping his eyes, Tim realized that a few snowflakes were starting to fall. There were two voices.

A female police officer approached warily. "Are you armed? Where is the knife?" she demanded.

Tim, in his confused state, wondered how she knew about the knife. "I don't have a knife. I can't find the knife."

The officers were taking no chances, and they patted him down, but it was obvious that the man they had apprehended was no hardened criminal. "We are going to stand you up now," she informed him.

"Okay."

"We are going to walk over to the pavilion."

"Okay."

Tim heard more voices now. He was not alone any longer. On this barren, cold, snowy night in late fall, he had been delivered from his ramblings. He was safe now. Tim was being taken into the embrace of people who did not plan to let go of him for a very long time.

Around 2:10 A.M., Deputy April Diaz was dispatched to the area of the Devil's Bathtub. A male had called 911 and told the operator that he had killed his wife. Diaz received information from the dispatcher that the suspect was by the Devil's Bathtub and the victim was still in the car by the pond. Diaz recalled in her police report, "I was sitting in the village of Honeoye Falls over on Monroe Street. I advised the dispatcher that I was en route."

Because the police were investigating a murder, they assembled their necessary investigative team. Four units met at the horse barns for mounted police patrols, located on Pond Road at the western border of the park. Joining Deputy Diaz were Deputies Gary Carpino, Norman Klein, Steven Thomsen, Todd Sutherland, and John Watson. They drove the short distance to the Devil's Bathtub's lower parking lot and arrived at 2:16 A.M. Exiting their vehicles, they began walking toward the pavilion nearby. They did an initial foot search in the area, but the 911 caller was nowhere to be found.

In the stillness of the night they heard a noise coming from the upper area, which was gated off. It sounded like a person crying. In the pitch dark the deputies slowly walked up the hill. First the upper pavilion came into view, and then they discovered a male wearing dark clothing in the parking lot. He was kneeling on the asphalt, with his hands splayed out and his cell phone open on the ground in front of him. He was crying hysterically, repeating, "I'm sorry; I'm sorry."

Approaching cautiously, because they had no idea if the man had a weapon, the team ordered him to stay where he was and not move. In just eight short minutes after the police had arrived, Timothy Wells was handcuffed and taken into custody without incident by Deputies Diaz and Watson. When asked why Tim was handcuffed, Deputy Diaz later told the grand jury, "Well, for our safety, number one, because no matter what the circumstances were, he shouldn't be in the park because the park closed at eleven."

While Tim was being handcuffed, he repeated over and over, "I'm sorry. . . . I didn't mean it. . . . I love her very much." When Deputy Diaz asked where "she" was, Tim responded,

In the early-morning hours of December 1, 2009, the police discovered Tim next to this pavilion in Mendon Ponds County Park. (Police photo)

"She's down there. In the car . . . This was her favorite spot."

It was necessary for Deputies Diaz and Watson to lift Tim up, because in his weak and helpless state, he was unable to stand by himself. He was stumbling and swaying all over the place. Deputy Diaz detected a strong odor of alcohol. They noticed he was wearing a jacket with a RIT logo on it—clearly not the usual attire for a killer. He continued to cry and say how sorry he was. The police officers assisted him over to the pavilion so he could sit down and lean against one of the posts. He was so distraught he was unable to move on his own. Over and over he kept repeating, "I love her so much. This was her favorite place" and "I just couldn't . . . "

Deputies Carpino, Klein, Sutherland, and Thomsen began to look for the car containing the victim. Their flashlights now illuminated an opening in the woods, and as they walked toward it, they located the vehicle on the hillside leading down to Deep Pond. They cautiously approached the car and saw that no one was inside. As they headed around the Saturn's trunk, they observed that it was partly open. Deputy Klein looked inside and discovered, wrapped in a plastic green tarp, a body. He checked the small woman's neck for a pulse but found none.

With the murder victim located, Sgt. Craig Backus and Lt. Jeffrey Wagner were notified and responded. Detectives were called, because they now had a confirmed homicide. Using yellow crime-scene tape, the deputies proceeded to secure the Devil's Bathtub and the parking lot by Deep Pond.

Meanwhile, at the top of the hill, the police officers were still looking for the dog Tim Wells said he had killed. They returned to him and asked, "Where is your dog?"

"She is dead, over by the bench."

"What direction?"

He indicated toward the esker. "The bench over there."

"We can't find your dog."

"What? She's right over there by the bench."

The officers went off to search for the dog again, but in the pitch-black darkness, with the snow starting to flurry, they were not having any success. Plus, now that the woman's dead body had been found, they had a more pressing need: to book her killer.

Deputy Watson informed Tim, "We are going to put you in the car now."

"Did you find Riley?"

"Not yet."

"That doesn't make sense," Tim thought to himself. He was so tired. "How can they not find her?" Nothing was going the way he had planned. "It has ended—but I'm still here. That's not right."

The police later found Riley alive, close to where Tim believed he had killed her. Mercifully, it turned out that Tim had failed at this task as well.

They now had in custody a man who had admitted to killing his wife, and she had been found dead in a car down the hill, just as he said. Deputy Watson moved quickly to take the murderer to the police station. The police wanted to find out if Timothy Wells would confess in a formal statement, and the best time to do so was immediately. At 2:57 A.M., the defendant was placed in the back of a Monroe County Sheriff's Office patrol vehicle. They arrived at the county Public Safety Building at approximately 3:04, and Deputy Watson escorted the suspect upstairs to a fourth-floor interview room. In short order, Investigator Scott Walsh began an interrogation that stretched into the middle of the following afternoon.

In the meantime, an ambulance crew arrived at the Devil's Bathtub. David Conner, the paramedic, checked the female victim and did not see any obvious injuries. The marks on her neck showed up only later in the bright lights of the autopsy room. Christine was officially pronounced dead at the scene at 2:50 A.M.

The snowstorm that had been threatening all night finally descended in full force as crime-scene technician Steve Williams arrived to collect evidence. In the parking lot where Tim had been found, Deputy Diaz pointed out three items that had been left behind by the suspect: his tortoiseshell eyeglasses, his T-Mobile Motorola flip-style cell phone, and his black leather satchel, containing a wallet with credit cards and identification in the name of Timothy D. Wells. Williams meticulously photographed the items, then captured the overall layout of the upper parking lot and picnic pavilion area.

The technician headed next to the suspect's vehicle,

located a hundred yards east of the parking lot down the hill. The vehicle's license plate was noted—NY #APX6550—then the car, a 2002 blue Saturn four-door sedan. The vehicle was stuck in the mud on what appeared to be a hiking trail. The technician further observed that the front tires on the vehicle appeared to have been spinning in the mud while traveling up the hill as well.

The crime technician then turned to the trunk, which was slightly open. He saw the green polyethylene tarp, and when he opened it, he saw Christine's lifeless body. In his report, he wrote, "The body was that of a Caucasian female wearing a white cloth jacket, blue sweater, gray sweatpants, black socks, and black sneakers. The female was lying in a fetal type position across the width of the trunk facing the front of the vehicle."

Tim's Saturn got stuck in mud about a hundred yards from where he planned to hold his final death rituals. Just after midnight on December 1, 2009, it began snowing in the Devil's Bathtub. (Police photo)

The Monroe County Sheriff's Office collected crime-scene evidence at Mendon Ponds County Park. Meanwhile, Tim was undergoing interrogation in downtown Rochester. (Police photo)

After a few short minutes, a tow-truck driver arrived to pull the Saturn out of the mud. Once it had been brought back to the lower parking lot, the body was removed from the trunk and transported to the morgue.

Christine Sevilla's chilly, daylong imprisonment in the trunk of Tim's old clunker had finally ended. The homicide committed by her cultured husband had been exposed to the world at last. To the shock of all who knew them, the image of the perfect loving couple had been shattered.

Prof. Timothy Wells was going down for murder two.

CHAPTER 4

"SO GOOD, IT WAS WORRISOME"

In the first bleak days after Christine Sevilla's death, her family and friends searched for answers. How could a perfect marriage end in murder? Everyone knew that Tim was quiet and reserved. No one would have guessed he was so filled with rage that he would strangle Christine with his bare hands. "This has never been a whodunit," her sister-in-law Donna remarked. "It's always been a whydunit."

The answers to an inexplicable event today can often be found in the patterns of the past. Tim was not always the brooding older professor who fell by the wayside of his profession. He had started out quite differently, growing up in a stable nuclear family in the 1950s. He married while in college and became a successful businessman. Despite the appearance that everything was going right, however, he abruptly divorced his first wife. It turned out he'd been having affairs for years. Tim switched his profession in midlife and entered academia. In everything he did, he tried to live up to what was expected of him, but time after time his restless spirit sabotaged him.

There is a branch of psychoanalysis that believes that all adult conflicts can be traced back to a child's interactions with his parents, both good and bad. That explanation might not be entirely true in Tim's case. He did show, however, certain tendencies from the very beginning that would, over time, harden into the man he would become.

Timothy David Wells was born on September 20, 1952, into a medical family. His father, Thomas, was a doctor and his mother, Betty, was a psychiatric nurse in the public school system. He had two sisters, Judy and Marilee, who were seven

Tom and Betty Wells were married for more than sixty years before their deaths in 2013. They raised their four children in what youngest son James later told the Democrat and Chronicle *was a "completely normal and you could even say wholesome" household.* (Courtesy of Timothy D. Wells)

and six years older, and a younger brother, James, who was born six years after him. As James later told the *Democrat and Chronicle*, it was a "completely normal and you could even say wholesome" household.

During the early years of Tim's childhood, the family lived in Benton, a suburb of Cleveland, Ohio. His father was a partner in a private medical practice before Tim was born. Tom was afflicted by a severe hearing loss, and by the 1960s he wore hearing aids on both ends of his glasses. He was able to make out what was said only in a quiet setting, which was fine in his doctor's office. But if there was background noise, such as at a party, he was lost. For that reason his parents didn't socialize much, and Tim doesn't remember them ever having anyone over for dinner. The children followed their lead. Tim later said, "I don't remember any of us kids having friends over to our house. I remember going to friends' houses to play."

Bound by his handicap, his father was a reserved man who kept his emotions tightly in check. The family likes to tell a revealing story about a common dynamic that afflicts Wells men. They are not authentic to their needs. Their true feelings fester for years and then explosively emerge. In this story, Tom and the children dutifully ate the liver and onions that Betty regularly prepared, as liver was believed in the 1950s to be healthy. Decades later, after the children were grown and out of the house, Betty suggested one night that she would make this dish. To her utter shock, her husband suddenly expressed his longstanding revulsion and disdain for liver and onions. "No! I won't eat them! I hate them! And now that the kids are gone, I'm not going to eat them anymore!"

That sort of rigid self-control manifested itself in other ways. Tim remembered that his father hardly ever got angry. The clinical demeanor with which he treated patients at the office was almost always maintained at home. Usually the only change he showed was becoming stern when he was disobeyed. Tim noted that if his father did start to become angry or frustrated, Betty would pull him aside to another room. She had training in psychology, after all. "They would come back and be in concord about the situation. I never saw or heard my parents fight or argue."

Tim recalled an incident when he was nine. "I'd have sore throats a couple times a year, and if it got bad enough, being a doctor and a nurse, they'd give me some penicillin. I remember hating it. They would sterilize the needle in boiling water on the stove, and you could smell the glass and the metal, so you knew it was coming. One time, I threw a tantrum, and my father grabbed me by the arm and said,

'You have to relax. It will hurt more if you fight.' So I did relax. He gave me the shot in the rump, and it hurt."

Tim recalled a similar incident while traveling to a family gathering. "I got this horrible headache in the car. I was throwing a tantrum: 'It hurts; it hurts; it hurts!' I remember my dad turning to me and saying, 'You have to calm down. It's not going to get better unless you calm down.' I remember while they unpacked the car, I stayed lying down in the backseat, and amazingly, the headache went away and I got up."

Tim's father was teaching him a lesson. Showing emotions, particularly strong, angry emotions, was unacceptable and unhealthy. For Tim, doing the wrong thing—exhibiting anger—never came to mind. It was never an option. He recalled, "Discipline was a firm command. It was never a struggle or question to do the right thing. Mom and Dad were so happy and proud when they were pleased, disappointed and concerned when they were not. I couldn't imagine doing the wrong thing."

Everyone in the family knew how well Tim took marching orders. He was very good at fitting in. Even as a child he was quiet and shy. He played with the other children in the neighborhood, but he didn't have best friends. When Christine later came on the scene, she talked to his mother during one family visit, asking what Tim was like as a little boy. Betty responded, "He was so good, it was worrisome."

Holding in emotions was a trait shared by the entire family. They were not given to displays of emotion. Unlike in more demonstrative families, there was very little hugging or kissing, no exclamations of "I love you!" Tim saw his mother and father kissing each other only occasionally, and they hardly ever hugged. They were reserved toward their children as well. Tim recalled that his mother kissed him, but his father neither kissed nor hugged him until he became an adult, and even then the welcoming hug seemed formal and perfunctory.

In a family so reserved, it is not surprising that they didn't say much about what was bothering them. "I talked with my aunt Ruth a lot about this," Tim reflected. "Our family just didn't tell each other about anything." One very big secret would be withheld from Tim until he was in his thirties. During the years before Tim was born, his father developed an addiction to a prescription drug, an amphetamine. The problem grew so bad he was forced to give up his private practice or face bankruptcy and public embarrassment for his obvious failure.

During the first few years of Tim's life, his father worked for the Veterans Administration in their Cleveland field office. The Wells family subsequently moved to Arlington, Virginia, after Tom was appointed to the Board of Veterans Appeals in Washington, D.C. as a senior medical officer. Each appeal was investigated and heard by a team of two lawyers and a physician. Dr. Wells would review military records and documents from veterans' claims, then render an opinion. During his long stint in the nation's capital, he would work either alone in his office or in a quiet hearing chamber.

The family moved into a white brick suburban house on a quiet street in Arlington. Although it was large enough for the family of six, the house did have one severe drawback. As Tim joked, "With Mom, Dad, and four kids in a one-bathroom house, the bathroom door was never closed. Two or three of us were in there at any given time—bathing, shaving, on the toilet."

Tim felt that his family was normal in most respects. "I have great memories of Dad teaching me to play tennis, chess, throwing a baseball." They ate dinner together every night. They were members of the nearby Evangelical United Brethren Church, and Tim and his mother sang in the

choir. One activity that the whole family grew to love was the
summer camping vacation, complete with the station wagon,
luggage rack, tent, and backpacks. Tim enjoyed these trips
very much. "In high school, I have fond memories of several
backpack hikes along the Appalachian Trail. Some with Dad,
Marilee or Judy, and me. Some just Dad and me."

Judy, the responsible oldest child, was a very good student
and involved in school activities. She went off to college and
married a Methodist minister. Marilee, a year younger, was
the rebellious child. She was not a good student and routinely
found boyfriends her father disliked.

Tim tells a story about one boyfriend who was so obnoxious
his father actually lost his temper. "I can remember Dad
yelling. I was upstairs in bed and they were downstairs.
Apparently, Marilee's date was doing something that made
my dad really angry, and my dad threw him out of the
house. The boy was in the front yard yelling at the house,
'But Marilee loves me!'" Tim recalled being startled and
wondering, "How would I handle this?" He heard the boy's
motorcycle roaring away, and a few minutes later his mother
opened his bedroom door and said, "It'll be all right," and
closed it again. As with many future conflicts in Tim's life,
he learned that by shrinking from them he could avoid
confronting the immediate threat.

His father's trials with his younger daughter weren't
over, though. She got a summer job, and one night when
she was walking home, she passed a seedy bar and a man
started following her. As she was turning onto her secluded
suburban street, the man tried to grab her. Tim recalled,
"She struggled, and she fell through a bush but managed to
pound on the door of a neighbor who lived down the street.
Her assailant ran away."

The neighbor brought frightened Marilee home, and Tom

exploded. "Dad starts off out the door to the street. Mom turns to me and says, 'Go with him.' So I do, and he's really, really angry and he is going to find whoever it was." Tim told himself that he didn't know how they would ever identify the man, but at a visceral level, his true concern was the impending confrontation. Many years later, Tim compared it to the same shrinking feeling he had when Christine challenged a motorcyclist in front of their house. "It was like, 'Oh, no. *Oh, no.'*" He nervously laughed as he remembered the scene at the bar, where his father had been heading. "I kept thinking, 'I'm not an intimidating person,' and I was standing in front of these guys."

Nor was his father much of a threat. Although he was six feet tall, he had only an average build, and he wore glasses. "He looked like a doctor," Tim commented. Yet he got his point across, because Marilee was never bothered again. After high school, she continued to rebel, participating in sixties countercultural events like Woodstock, but eventually she settled down, attending nursing school.

Tim went on to public high school in Arlington. He excelled in his studies, especially in math, and in 1970 he graduated at the top of his class. He was a good kid who was involved in a variety of activities. Being tall was an asset in sports, but as a child he wasn't very athletic. He remembered, "In gym class, I was never picked first but seldom the last." He had had a growth spurt at the end of seventh grade, shooting up to six foot three. In basketball, which he played scholastically from seventh to ninth grades, he started one year but then was relegated to second string. He also made the track team, and during junior high he was a star in the high jump, tying the county high-jump record. By the end of eighth grade he had reached an athletic plateau but continued participating in sports until the middle of his senior year. A conflict of

Tim's high-school senior photo, 1970. During high school, Tim auditioned for act-ing and singing groups that would put him in front of his classmates. He was surprised to find he was welcomed by many groups: "It was a great year." (Courtesy of Timothy D. Wells)

interest gradually developed between athletics and his evolving passion for music. "In twelfth grade, the track coach was upset that I was missing morning practice in favor of choir rehearsals. He gave me an ultimatum. I think he was surprised when I turned in my uniform."

As with so many facets of adolescence, Tim's interests were determined to a certain degree by whether he was accepted by other students. "In high school I was never in the popular crowds. I knew people and got along but had no best friends," he related. "In my senior year things changed some. I tried out and was chosen for the twelve-singer group called the Madrigals." He was selected because of his fine voice, an alto that his first wife loved. He also participated in several plays. In his first one, he landed the lead in Tennessee Williams' *Summer and Smoke.* In addition, as part of a drama class, he put on a one-person show made up of songs and soliloquies. "These put me in front of the school," he remembered, "and I found I was welcome in more groups. The Madrigals group was very close knit. It was a great year."

For a boy who always did what he was told, his choice of college was easy: Otterbein College, in Ohio. Both his parents had gone there, and with his excellent grades, he was readily accepted. All was going smoothly and according to plan. Unexpectedly he became unraveled during the summer following his senior year. "I got really anxious about going off to college," he said. He was participating in a summer retreat of his evangelical church's youth group. In one session he began crying hysterically, saying that he just didn't know what to do. A church counselor told him, "Tim, I don't understand. You have already been accepted to college. You are going off to college." Tim refused to be consoled, however. It was a rare but telling lapse for a young man who kept his emotions tightly in check. Nor would it be the last time Tim collapsed under stress.

Otterbein is located in Westerville, Ohio, just north of the state capital of Columbus and not far from Croton, where his father grew up on a farm. Tim intended to major in music, with the idea of going on to become a music teacher. He played guitar and mandolin in productions of *Camelot* and *Fiddler on the Roof.* He also had a walk-on part in *Romeo and Juliet.* Yet the interests he had carried with him out of high school would change during the fall of his sophomore year. The college, which has long emphasized community involvement and global engagement, offered a number of study-abroad options. One of them featured a semester on a converted cruise ship, and there he would meet the first love of his life.

The World Campus Afloat program was affiliated with Chapman University in Orange County, California. On September 3, 1971, nearly three hundred college students from thirty-eight states and eight foreign countries joined seventy faculty members and staff aboard the SS *Atlantic* for a unique four-month trip abroad. Departing Los Angeles, the students visited such places as Honolulu, Bali, Singapore, Sri Lanka, Bombay, and Cape Town, South Africa. They stayed at each port for four or five days at a time. They were scheduled to visit Casablanca as a final foreign port of call, but the ship struck a dock in Freetown, Sierra Leone, and the resulting hole had to be patched with cement. With the hull in such an unstable condition, the ship instead headed for the Canary Islands and on to New York, arriving just days before Christmas.

While aboard, Tim stayed in a private, rather Spartan cabin. Classes were taught from 8:00 A.M. to 6:00 P.M., six days a week. As a music major with a political-science minor, he took courses on Music of the World, Comparative Governments, the United Nations, and Comparative Education Systems. When they were not touring the ports that they visited, they had to write reports and carry out special assignments. Tim also gained the role of the Boy, a character who embraced the innocence of youth, in the musical *The Fantasticks.* Many years later, Tim would re-audition for a different theatre group performing *The*

Fantasticks and this time would land the lead part, El Gallo.

Tim also displayed his musical talent as a performer. Accompanying himself on his acoustic guitar, he sang for the other students during the semester's first talent show, near the end of their journey together. He chose to sing these self-composed lyrics:

Many a long and dusty mile I've traveled from my home.
Seems like there's a million more to go
Back to the faces I left smiling and their places in my past
Sunny days and nights so long ago.

Mom is in the kitchen fix'n up the evening meal.
The sun shines through the window in the hall.
Dad is reading in the den
And James and me come running in.
Scenes like that I frequently recall.

And each mile I sail away
My home comes closer to me
And then they say, I am far away.
I know that they can't fool me for I know I will be home
To see that Yule-time log turn to flame.

Once I sailed across the northern sea for my travels.
I did find good friends who treated me kind.
Home is where this boy is bound to be.

Many fellow students, who by this time were also homesick, started crying as he played. This was when his future wife Carrie first noticed him. She came up to Tim right after the show and said how much she liked his singing. "She looked at me with such desire," Tim remembered, "I was flabbergasted. I think it was the next night that we slept together." Carrie later referred to this as his James Taylor period, the folk star whom he emulated both in

voice and choice of songs. Carrie was attracted to his gentle, quiet nature, and she fell in love with him. By the end of the cruise, they vowed to continue their romance.

This was the first time Tim had ever had a girlfriend. He was never very good at dating and all through high school viewed girls as friends. "I never felt comfortable being assertive the way I saw other men, other boys, being," he said. "I often wondered, 'Why is that girl going with him when she could be going with me?' But then you think, 'I haven't done anything; I haven't put myself forward.'"

Trying to help out, his older sister Marilee gave her brother lessons on how to ask a girl for a date. She would say things like, "Be specific and give the girl a way out." Rather than asking, "Are you doing anything Saturday night?" he should say, "Do you want to go with me to the game?" Tim didn't like the advice very much. Because he was shy and gentle, he got confused when girls seemed to prefer boys who treated them badly. "A lot of girls saw me as a

In college, Tim seemed to have it all. He was bright, talented, and musical. He sang a number of James Taylor songs and even tried to look like him. (Courtesy of Carrie Wells)

nice guy and a friend but not someone you dated."

As a senior in high school, he became infatuated with a sophomore named Patty Woodson. "She was a part of the party group and I wanted to get into that group," he recalled, "but she kept me at a distance from her friends. I once asked her about it and she told me I just wouldn't fit in." She did like him, because he was such a nice guy. They often kissed and petted, but when she said "enough," he stopped. She felt she could trust him not to pressure her about having sex. She was right, but Tim had a lot of testosterone he was holding back.

All that changed after he met Carrie. In fall 1972, he kept his promise to continue their romance by transferring to the college she was attending, Eastern Washington University. Located in Cheney, it was close to the border with Idaho, where her parents had a ranch.

Tim made another significant change. He switched his major from music to mathematics, the closest a student could come to computer science at most universities back then. His high school hadn't offered computer-science courses, and the facilities for computer training were limited at Otterbein. "One of the required math courses had a short section on computers," he recalled about Otterbein. "The college had one teletype terminal connected to a mainframe at Ohio State in Columbus. I was able to spend some time on it writing BASIC programs." Eastern

Tim worked as a ranch hand for Carrie's parents during the first summer of their courtship. (Courtesy of Carrie Wells)

Washington University, by contrast, offered many computer-science courses at that time, involving language, operating systems, data structures, and math and computing principles.

His thinking was that music teachers were a dime a dozen, and if he followed that career, he would never make much money—if he could even get a job. He wanted to please Carrie, and he decided to go into computer science as a profession. He believed that this field held greater financial promise.

Looking back, Tim regretted taking that fork in the road. "I don't like the idea of playing 'What if?' games, but I keep coming back to, 'What if I had stayed on the track that I had been on to become a professional music teacher?'" His best friend at the time, Greg Bauder, asked him over and over, "Why are you doing this?" Yet Tim felt he had to do right by Carrie, since they were about to get married.

Their wedding took place on August 23, 1973, the summer after he transferred to Eastern Washington University. It was a big wedding, held at the Idaho Methodist Church in Kellogg, Idaho. Carrie had four bridesmaids and a maid of honor. A large contingent of Tim's extended family came. Carrie joked afterward that the wedding took place in her town, but his side of the church was full.

Carrie was ecstatic about marrying such a tall, handsome man. "She liked showing me off as the husband she imported from the East," Tim remarked. "She often referred to our 'shipboard romance.'" The following year, Tim completed his bachelor's degree in mathematics. He was well positioned to pursue a career in the rapidly developing world of computers.

After finishing his undergraduate studies, Tim took a job as a computer programmer at Bunker Hill, a mining company located an hour east of Kellogg. The young couple lived in a permanent trailer on her parents' ranch. The pattern of their marriage was the same as it would be with Christine, Tim later commented. Both of Tim's wives provided his social

Tim and Carrie were married in Idaho in 1973. (Courtesy of Deni Linhart, Fine Image Photography)

sphere, as they each had large groups of friends. He relied upon each of them as his primary source of love and fun and friendship. In turn, both Carrie and Christine colluded with Tim to avoid conflict. Tim commented on the unspoken deal he accepted: "I could be the nice guy. In return, I was happy to do what I could to make them happy. I felt horrible if I thought they were disappointed in me." Tim's marriages appeared to be free of conflict, but just beneath the surface, more malignant dynamics were unfolding.

Like Christine, Carrie was strong-willed to the point that her beliefs didn't always bring about the desired outcome. Tim recalled an incident shortly after their wedding that he felt was indicative of their marriage. "Our car muffler broke. We drove to a shop that advertised some special deal. After getting the car on the rack, the mechanic said the price would be higher. Carrie told off the mechanic and insisted that we go somewhere else, where we ended up paying more than the previous estimate." Tim learned that keeping quiet had its price.

With this arrangement, these years were happy ones for Carrie. Tim was her best friend. They had a house filled with dogs and cats and a parakeet. Carrie wistfully remembered how kind, gentle, sweet, caring, and articulate Tim was. People who knew them, she recalled, referred to them as having the "perfect marriage." Carrie remembered that they argued only twice in the whole time they were married. Later, in her vain effort to persuade Tim to stay with her, she pointed out to him, "We are supposed to have years of fighting and arguments before we divorce!"

A major reason for Carrie's happiness was Tim's refusal to get mad. "The only emotion Tim hated was anger," Carrie observed. Tim agreed, saying, "Anger is a foreign thing to me. I never liked the feeling." Right after college, though, the young couple was broke, living on tuna fish and macaroni and cheese. At times, Carrie was short-tempered, and he would call her out on it. "Of course, his anger was civilized and quiet," Carrie remarked. "I knew him well enough that I could tell when he was pissed off." That was how rigidly he controlled himself; only Carrie could detect it. "Others wouldn't have seen it unless they knew him *very* well." On the contrary, Carrie commented, "he disliked conflict so much he would allow people to walk over him with spikes."

Over the course of their long marriage, she could remember only a half-dozen occasions when he showed even a hint of anger. She recalled one time when Tim actually flew into a rage, with fatal consequences. Their parakeet escaped from its cage one day, and their Persian cat, Big Boy, caught the bird in its mouth. Tim grabbed Big Boy by the tail in an ill-conceived effort to save their parakeet and swung the cat around so hard that the bird flew out of Big Boy's mouth. The only problem was that the bird crashed into the wall and was killed instantly. Big Boy, uninjured, bolted from Tim's grasp.

As a couple, they decided to have no children. Tim stated the reason was that Carrie did not want to have any. "I think I would have been a good parent. With Carrie, it didn't seem right. She said she was not anxious to have children. She worried about the X-ray radiation she had been exposed to as a veterinary assistant. She said she couldn't imagine herself as a mother. There was no pressure from her parents because her two brothers wanted to have children." Carrie remembered the opposite, that Tim didn't want them. Later, he got a vasectomy, because he didn't like using a condom for birth control.

For seven years, Tim worked as a computer programmer. During the 1970s, Bunker Hill was the nation's second-largest lead smelter, producing nearly one-fifth of the processed lead in the world. The gigantic amounts of lead dust emitted during the smelting filled the air and lands around the factory for miles. Combined with the toxic mine and smelter tailings, its deadly pollution resulted in its being forced to shut down. In 1983, the Environmental Protection Agency declared the mine a Superfund cleanup site.

By that time, though, Tim had left the job behind. He felt he needed more business training in order to make more money, so he decided to get a master's in business administration. He found both a job and an MBA program in Bakersfield, California. "Carrie was not happy about the idea of leaving Idaho. I felt badly about asking her." He promised that if they went to California, he would complete the MBA program in less than two years. "Then we could move back to the ranch and build a house."

They lived in an apartment in Bakersfield, a hot, dusty city about one hundred miles north of Los Angeles. While Tim attended classes at California State University at Bakersfield, he worked as a supervisor of systems and programming at a manufacturing company named Hopper, Inc. As he neared completion of the MBA in 1980, he began looking for ways to move back to Idaho. Bunker Hill by this time had gone out of business. The area held out very few prospects, so he took an offer to join a software consulting company called Yourdon, Inc. Based in New York, it was opening an office in San Francisco. Although the job involved a lot of travel, he thought that he might be able to move back to Idaho once he proved himself in San Francisco, or he could start his own consulting business and work out of Idaho. A friend of Carrie's had moved to a town north of San Francisco, so they rented a house near him, and Tim started his consulting career.

A year later, the owner of the company, Ed Yourdon, allowed Tim to relocate to Idaho and fly out of nearby

Tim posed somberly with Carrie, his first wife, upon earning his MBA in 1980. (Courtesy of Carrie Wells)

Spokane, Washington. Tim was uneasy about returning to Idaho, but he had promised Carrie they would. They settled back into the trailer on her parents' ranch. Tim headed off to work, quickly becoming a top seminar instructor and requested consultant. Yet his heart wasn't in his new profession.

In between all of the business trips he was taking, Tim found the time to write four books. "I hoped that by getting into writing," he noted, "that would allow me to make enough money to eventually quit the consulting business. I knew that was a long shot." His first book, published in 1982, had the technical title of *Tie Failure Rate Analysis and Prediction Techniques.* That was followed by three books relating to the early languages of computer-programming code. *A Structured Approach to Building Programs: BASIC* appeared in 1985, followed by *A Structured Approach to Building Programs: COBOL* a few months later. Another year passed before the third in the series, *A Structured Approach to Building Programs: Pascal,* was published.

Carrie was proud of his success. "I wanted people to see his talents. I pushed him and promoted him," she recalled. She made him feel good because she admired him so. She was aware, however, that her brilliant husband was a computer nerd. Watching him at parties, Carrie saw that he disconnected from what was going on around him. "Tim often stepped outside of himself," she noted. "He would actually be present but not engaged, as if he were watching from a distance."

His detachment went much further than Carrie realized. Although he was a model husband, he was still playing a role. He laughed as he recalled during a later jail interview, "I was pretty good at it!" Inside, however, he was profoundly dissatisfied with the way his life was turning out. He remembered thinking, "I am doing all the right things. Why don't I feel good?"

His natural tendency to act according to what people expected of him fed into his love for performing. When they returned from California, Carrie urged him to join a community theatre group. "I felt uneasy about it because my schedule was so uncertain," he recalled. "I had to schedule vacation time or make special arrangements to ensure I

wouldn't be called to a consulting assignment during the last
week of rehearsal and several performances." He played the
lead in Oscar Wilde's *The Importance of Being Earnest*. Tim also
played the lead in a community-theatre favorite, *The Little
Shop of Horrors*. He acted in plays written by local playwrights
as well, including one called *The First Hundred Years*. Carrie
wryly commented about the amateurish effort, "I think the
name referred to how long it seemed to last."

The second time Tim acted in *The Fantasticks*, he played
the cynical, godlike narrator, El Gallo, a sharp contrast to
his previous role as the Boy. In one particularly bittersweet
passage, El Gallo reflects on the angst of maturing from
the naivety of childhood to the cynicism of adulthood.
He believes that the critical lessons of life require that

In Tim's second go-round with The Fantasticks, *then in his thirties, he played the
lead part of El Gallo, dressed all in black.* (Courtesy of Carrie Wells)

we all must be "burned"—hurt, destroyed, consumed. El Gallo prophesizes that life is never truly complete until we have all been burned. Tim's role as El Gallo portended his own fate.

Carrie believed that Tim was drawn to the stage because it allowed him to take on different personas with little risk of reprisal. For example, he could be El Gallo, a cynical, dark character. Not only was this okay, but he was applauded for his talent. Tim, with his excellent acting skills, was able to take leave of his identity and become someone else with little effort. She added sourly, "Maybe Tim learned more about playing roles through his roles."

Carrie was referring to another role that he played in real life, one in which he was not the shining knight at all. On his frequent business trips, Tim was surprised to find that a tall, thin man with a mustache and dark good looks could attract women. Toward the end of his work with Yourdon, most of his assignments were one-week seminars or consulting engagements. He began to notice that certain women he was working with in the seminars were paying particular attention to him. Tim mused, "I felt good about that. I have to believe that that had always been the case, but I didn't notice that until the end and I began responding."

These women knew that Tim was married, and he never made any promises, but that's not what they wanted in any case. The women, not Tim, initiated the affairs. According to him, each woman needed affirmation that she was still attractive, and he was convenient. He didn't have to do anything. "In all the cases, I didn't feel like I was the person pursuing it, but I was really happy that it was happening. Safe and short-term adventures."

The first of the affairs put Tim between a woman and her partner. Tim recalled, "She was actually a woman who

was breaking up with her boyfriend. I found that out later."
During a seminar, she approached him and asked, "Are you
new in town? Because if you don't know any place to stay, I
can help." Tim replied, "Well, you can suggest some places."
They had sex that night.

The next night, they went out. She told him, "I have a
place to go for a drink and a late dinner." Tim was happy to
go along, but he should have suspected an ulterior motive.
"It turned out that at the place there was a band playing, and
the bass player was her ex-boyfriend. So it was clear she was
using me to say, 'Hey, I'm okay without you.' And I was fine
with that." He laughed at this point in the story. "I found this
out in retrospect, which was good because he was a pretty big
guy. And I'm not a very tough person."

Unlike many married men who feel so guilty that they
break down and confess to their wives, Tim wanted out of
his marriage. Over the years, Carrie had put on weight, and
she was no longer attractive to him. When he thought back
on the affairs, the word "affirmed" came to his mind. "I felt
flattered that I was attractive. So, I look back at those business
affairs with no guilt. No guilt with Carrie." He compared it to
movies when one member of a couple asks, "How can you do
this to me?" "Every time I see a movie like that, I stop and say,
'No, that's wrong.' I did it for me."

Over a three-year period, Tim had no less than seven affairs.
Five of them were related to the business trips, flings of very
short durations. Given how cloaked Tim's inner life was from
the eyes of others, he had no problem keeping his liaisons
from his wife. Carrie had no inkling of what was going on. She
thought they had a great sex life. She almost stumbled onto
the truth on one occasion, however. They were chatting, and
he made a reference to seeing a corkboard made from wine
corks. Long afterward, she realized that this was something

he must have seen with a paramour in New Mexico. She noted, "There were clues, but I did not see them. He did not want to hurt me, in some strange, twisted way."

Two of Tim's more serious affairs involved local partners. Both of these women were married, which gave Tim and his lovers a degree of safety. One relationship lasted for a year, the other for a year and a half. Over time, Tim started to develop strong feelings for each of them, to the point that he entertained thoughts of leaving Carrie. Yet the first woman, Lindsey, ended their affair abruptly by leaving town.

Tim began his second more serious affair with Terri during a production of *The Little Shop of Horrors* that Carrie directed. Terri was a cast member. At first, they kidded around and flirted some. He recalled, "But the way she looked at me was so exciting. One day I asked if she wanted to have lunch sometime. She didn't want to go anywhere where people might see us, so I suggested having a picnic in a nearby park. There were several secluded areas. I remember that day with joy. I was leaning against a tree looking at the lake. Terri came up from behind and kissed me."

She then asked Tim, "Should we do this?" He immediately said yes but told Terri he didn't plan to leave Carrie, nor did he want to take her away from her husband. She asked Tim if it was her, or could it be any girl? Tim said, "Perhaps, if she was just like you—as pretty and confident and looked at me the way you do." This day felt magical to Tim. It so affirmed him to know that she desired him.

From that day on, Tim and Terri searched for ways to be together. The two illicit lovers became close to the point that Tim even said, "She was the only person that I ever felt like I wanted to have children with." In the end, though, she decided to focus on her husband.

During this affair, Tim made a casual statement that surprised Carrie. While they were having a conversation, he absentmindedly said, "It would be nice to have kids." Carrie described this as a total reversal from his position throughout their marriage.

By this time, Tim had lost sexual interest in Carrie. "During the last year of our marriage, we seldom had sex," he noted, "and Carrie always initiated it. It felt like an obligation." Still, he had not stopped going through the motions of loving her. He had never felt passionately about her, but he was comfortable in his marriage. It was what he believed he should do. Besides, as Carrie pointed out, he could never confront her and say he was unhappy. "He could barely get half a sentence out, it was so hard for him."

In the months just before the end of their marriage, Tim became increasingly bold in his sexual encounters. Carrie recalled a jaunt to a small town near their home where a Christmas pageant with music was being presented in the outdoor square. Tim left to buy an airline ticket from a travel agent. He was gone for an hour, and he returned with the travel agent, smiling and laughing. Carrie had the distinct feeling that they had just had sex but denied the possibility. After she and Tim separated, the husband of the travel agent called Carrie and informed her that his soon-to-be ex-wife was a cheat and had had many affairs.

That was not the only incident. Soon after that, Carrie asked to go on a business trip with him, and too quickly he said no. Carrie thought this was very odd, and she asked, "You're not thinking about divorcing me, are you?" Tim put her off with a simple no.

The end of the marriage was near. Tim later said, "At that point I felt like I was broken and I didn't want to be fixed." He wanted a new life, and yet he was bound to his old one. "I had never thought of life without Carrie, but these relationships challenged that. I was very frightened and confused. Looking back, I was confused because I did not know what I wanted. I wanted to make Carrie happy, but the harder I tried, the worse I felt."

In March of 1986, while they were driving to Spokane on an errand, Carrie talked about a conference she had just attended. Suddenly, Tim blurted out, "I want a divorce," and he started crying hysterically. Alarmed by this outburst, she directed him to pull off the highway.

Once he had parked on the shoulder, he told her, "I don't love you anymore."

She asked, "Were you lying when you said you loved me?"

He replied, "I have not loved you for the past two years."

To this day she is saddened by "the way he killed our marriage—I was too old and fat and ugly."

Tim confessed that he had been having an affair for eleven months, but his lover had just broken up with him. Carrie soon found out there were other affairs as well. "He had been living a double life. It came to a head and he just left," she recalled. Carrie was stunned, and she was hardly alone. When she informed her parents that Tim wanted a divorce, they were completely surprised. "That was how cloaked his emotions were."

As Carrie talked in retrospect about learning of Tim's other affairs, she made an interesting comment. "He had created a whole separate Tim, a Tim that had girlfriends . . . a whole other life." She noted how skilled Tim was in covering up these multiple affairs. He was "excellent at concealing a whole other world."

In less than two weeks, Tim moved out of the house, with no talk of reconciliation. When he left, he walked away from everything—their home, their marriage, the life they had built together. Despite Carrie's desperate efforts to reconcile, Tim was done with her.

In a one-and-a-half-page typewritten letter dated November 9, 1987, Tim explained to Carrie, in a distant, intellectualized voice, why he saw no future for them. His second sentence asserted, "I find it hard to define an objective or purpose for the letter." He continued, "It's hard to avoid semantics that fix blame, or that tend to rationalize. I find myself on the defensive with only two choices, admitting that I am a bad person and trying to make amends, or saying that I'm glad it all happened and I'll probably do it all again." In his final bleak rejection of Carrie, Tim admitted, "I already turned away from you in pursuit of romance. So, it is obvious that I am willing to give up the relationship we had." Tim concluded his letter with the ironic resolve "to deal with conflict and relationships more honestly."

He also insisted that he divorce her rather than have her divorce him. Even so, Carrie did not feel that their divorce was acrimonious. It was finalized on August 8, 1988.

In hindsight, Carrie referred to Tim's persona during their marriage as "Two-world Tim: Romeo marauding traveling salesman Tim, and Tim the family man." In those final years together, she believes, "These two Tims were on a collision course. He was unraveling." She referred once again to the role-playing he did so well. "Each part of Tim was genuine. In each role he was very convincing, even after our thirteen years together."

"Two-world Tim" would not change after he fled his first marriage. The ugly pattern would repeat itself with his second wife, Christine Sevilla. Christine's brother similarly said years later, at the time of Tim's sentencing, "He lived the last year or two a double life, emotionally, because he completely hid to everybody this sense of complete failure that he expressed to the court." While Tim was descending in his long journey to an inner hell, Christine had not a clue. In the end, he believed he had to kill her to keep her from discovering his other, damaged world.

CHAPTER 5

FIRE AND RAIN

After the explosive breakup on the shoulder of the
highway, Tim Wells was cast adrift. He had been married
nearly fifteen years, and he felt as if he were leaving home,
only he was not a child anymore. He moved to nearby
Spokane and continued to travel for his job. Yet nothing felt
the same. For the next two months, he saw a psychologist
to talk about the issues related to his marital problems and
divorce. During the course of his counseling, he came to
see his extramarital affairs in a new light. He had married at
such an early age, and Carrie was his first sexual partner. The
affairs, he realized, made up for experiences he never had in
high school and college. What the counseling did not reveal,
and what Tim did not understand until many years later, was
that his affairs satisfied a deep longing from his youth, the
need to be wanted by women. The problem was that these
affairs cost him his marriage.

He continued to feel obligated to support Carrie. "That
sense of doing what I should lasted well after the divorce. I
continued to pay the mortgage, taxes, property and health
insurance for two years after I left. I never considered trying
to sell the house, because it was not my house. My father
encouraged me to try to split the assets, but I could not bring
myself to even consider it."

Tim's parents were surprised by the divorce. There had
been no sign of any trouble for nearly fifteen years. At the
time of the wedding, they worried that Tim was too young
and fell in love too soon after his infatuation with his high-
school flame, Patty. All those years later, Tim placed a call to
them a week after telling Carrie he wanted a divorce.

Away on a business assignment, Tim called home from his hotel. He recalled, "Mom answered as usual. I said I wanted to talk to Dad. She was surprised and asked what was the problem. I repeated that I needed to talk to Dad. I knew he would have a lot of trouble hearing but for some reason I couldn't tell Mom." Tim thought his father would understand. The men in the Wells family did not show their feelings. When his father came on the line, Tim had to almost yell into the phone because his father had so much trouble hearing.

They didn't talk long. His father remarked that he had no idea things were so bad. "That startled me because I could see that from his standpoint (and everyone else's) things weren't bad." His father asked if he wanted to come home. Tim arranged a short visit soon after. "During that visit, Mom tried to comfort and understand," he recalled. "She said that she knew all along that 'I was the giving one.' That comment also startled me. I hadn't thought of one being only giving and the other always taking. I hadn't conceived of our relationship like that. It just was."

During that year in Spokane, Tim dated a woman who lived in the same apartment complex. She ended up asking for a more serious relationship, but he was too unsettled to consider it.

Tim might have remained unmoored in eastern Washington for some time, but fate was to return him to the East Coast. The company he worked for, Yourdon, Inc., was bought up by Kodak, the camera giant whose headquarters are located in Rochester, New York. Tim gladly accepted an offer to relocate back East, bringing him closer to where all of his family still lived.

Tim was being given a second chance at happiness. He no longer lived a continent apart from his family. Now he needed a partner he could merge with, one who could make him complete. That woman turned out to be a fiery, twice-divorced hospital administrator from the West Coast, the area he had just left behind.

Christine Diane Sevilla was born in 1951 in Sunnyvale, California, in the heart of what later become Silicon Valley. A bubbly little girl with Shirley Temple curls and deep-blue eyes, she was the baby of the family, with two much older brothers, Charles (Chuck) and Michael. Her grandparents were first-generation immigrants from Spain. Her father worked at Westinghouse, and her stay-at-home mother brought up the children. Christine later wrote that her Spanish-speaking family caused her to feel different from her classmates. "During my California childhood, my family's Spanish language and culture surrounded me, and I felt unlike other children in the context of a 'superior' Anglo culture. Friends commented that coming to my house was unlike visiting other homes."

Like her future husband, Christine was obedient when she was younger. Yet even as a child she was very gutsy. She told Tim a story of how her bicycle was once stolen by a biker gang. A few days later, she saw her bike parked on the porch of a house where the gang lived. She walked right up to the porch and took back her bike.

According to Chuck, nine years her senior, the three children grew up healthy and had good educations. "Following high school, when Christine left for college at University of California at Santa Barbara, she was so young but eager to take part in the world around her." She would earn her bachelor's degree in anthropology.

Christine's high-school sweetheart, Paul Malatesta, attended the same college, and the two married in 1973, a few months after she graduated. The plan was for Paul to attend graduate school while Christine worked, and then they would reverse roles. The two moved East when Paul was accepted into the Simon School of Business at the University of Rochester, where he earned a master's and later a Ph.D. in management. Christine found employment selling cosmetics at a J. C. Penney's store in the Pittsford Plaza, located in an affluent suburb in Rochester. Her coworker at the time and longtime friend, Betty Nolan, remembered Christine's marriage to Paul as troubled. Betty told the *Democrat and Chronicle,* "She became strong later. She wasn't like that then."

Paul, who now teaches at the University of Washington in Seattle, said he found Christine childlike in many ways, a sentiment that Tim later echoed. "I blame myself for the failure of our marriage," Malatesta told reporters in Rochester. They separated during his third year of graduate school.

Christine's intrepid spirit kept her going, though. Immediately after the divorce, she headed back home to California. Her father gave her such a cold reception, however, that very shortly thereafter she returned to Rochester. She began working toward a master's degree in public administration at the State University of New York at Brockport. Meanwhile, she supported herself by waitressing at a Honeoye Falls restaurant and working at a camera shop in the Eastview Mall, which was close to her previous job at J. C. Penney's. Her job at the camera shop spawned her love for photography, which later became such a major part of her life.

Being artistic appealed to her in a number of ways. She started going to vintage stores and finding distinctive clothing, which she preferred over the latest fashions at Macy's. Christine even made many of her own clothes. Tim remembered that she liked to look atypical but not outlandish, and she loved getting compliments on her large wardrobe of colorful and comfortable clothing.

A mutual friend introduced Christine to Robert Zehler

several years after her divorce. Rob became her second husband in the early 1980s. They lived in Perinton, and he worked as a soundman for several local bands. Rob remembered, "Christine was a really creative person. She looked at everything as a photograph." Driven as ever, Christine earned her master's degree in 1985. However, the marriage soon reached an impasse: he wanted children and she didn't. That issue became further complicated when Christine had a hysterectomy. Her doctor found precancerous growths and advised the procedure. She went along with the advice, but she would come to regret her decision. After the surgery was completed, she became angry at "what they did" to her.

Just before they separated in 1988, a peculiar incident took place that eerily foreshadowed what would happen in her third marriage. They were having a picnic in the Genesee Valley Park, and as the story goes, Christine unpacked the basket and discovered Rob had secreted a gun amongst the items. He was quiet and distant. They finished their lunch and left. She said it was surreal because she sensed that Rob was contemplating killing her or both of them. This affirmed her conviction to divorce Rob. After her murder, Tim, aware of this story, couldn't help but contemplate its irony.

Single again, Christine became an administrator at Strong Memorial Hospital, now known as University of Rochester Medical Center. She managed their outpatient clinics there and also helped in the development of staff training. She was particularly gifted at creating better training and job procedures, and when the hospital staff resisted implementing her ideas, she characteristically became impatient with their inability to see the superiority of her ideas. By the time she met Tim, she was miserable there. She was very frustrated with her job and the environment. Tim confided that Christine tended to take on tasks without prior approval. She saw so many issues and problems that could be improved upon, but she was seldom able to implement her proposals. She would often come home mad and irritated. Tim worked hard to help her calm down.

Christine had better luck in finding a religious community she enjoyed. Ernie Lederman, one of her oldest friends in the area, said that at first she visited numerous places of worship. Even though she was raised as a Catholic, she briefly experimented with B'rith Kodesh in Brighton, a Jewish temple that Lederman's family belonged to. She eventually discovered the local First Unitarian Church. Abby Chodoff, a longtime church member and close friend of hers, remembered that she was prim and proper when she first attended services. Various chorus members urged Christine, a soprano, to join the church choir, which she did hesitantly because she thought her singing voice was off key. But Chodoff told the local paper, "She had a beautiful instrument. She just didn't know what to do with it."

Christine was beautiful and single, and soon her dark-brown curls and expressive face attracted the attention of another new member of the church, Tim Wells. He had become a Unitarian during his latter years out West, so switching to the church in Rochester was a natural transition. He went out with another woman from the Unitarian Church several times. She was looking for someone to care for her, but Tim was drawn to another member of the church. She was a fiery, demonstrative woman, who Tim recalled was energetic, opinionated, loyal, and warm. He joined the choir solely to make this woman's acquaintance. According to Chodoff, he had to compete for her attention with another suitor. But it didn't take long before Christine was making sweet music with tall, handsome, shy Tim Wells.

They were a match of opposites. Although Christine,

only five-foot-one, barely came up to Tim's shoulder, she was outgoing and outspoken. She felt she matched her astrological sign. "Leo is the best," she'd say with a big smile. Jeffrey Lasky, Tim's later department chair at RIT, was taken by her. He said, "If we could plug her into the grid, she'd power all of New York." She'd work through the wee hours of the morning if she needed to complete a project. For Tim, a committed dog lover, Christine came with one added bonus. She had a springer spaniel named Amanda, who was "her baby," he noted with approval.

Tim was the more aloof, withdrawn partner. Roger Wilhelm, former music director of the Madrigalia Chamber Singers, the church's other singing group that performed on special occasions, observed, "Tim was very, very even tempered. Sometimes I wondered if he really did like something, enjoy what he was doing, because he never showed extremes of emotions." On the other hand, Tim was just what fiery Christine needed.

Tim and Christine did not rush into new marriages. They went out for nearly two years before tying the knot. Part of the reason was Christine's reluctance about taking a partner who was so willing to do everything she said. Tim recalled one near breakup during this period. Several months earlier, he had moved into a house Christine had rented since she and her second husband had split up. "One day she was very serious and a little sad. She said she thought it best if I moved out," he recalled. "She said she wasn't sure she wanted our relationship to get any more serious. She said she couldn't tell what I wanted. That I just went along with what she wanted."

Always eager to please, Tim moved out but asked if they could continue seeing each other, and she agreed. He promised to display more backbone and told her he would try to give her "something to push against." For the next few weeks, they saw each other at church and went to lunch occasionally. Then he got a call late one night. Christine was having a bad asthma attack. He said he'd be right over.

She asked, "Do you really want to?"

He replied, "Yes, of course," and rushed to be by her side.

He found that she was very weak. He called her doctor and took her to the emergency ward, where she stayed overnight. A short time after that, she and Tim were back together.

During the same period, Tim's occupation changed. Kodak divested itself of Yourdon, and his company decided to move to North Carolina. They offered Tim a position in charge of seminar development. It sounded interesting, but Mr. Yourdon had left the company, and Tim did not like the new management team. He was also sure that he would be expected to travel a lot, despite assurances he wouldn't have to. He and Christine reluctantly went down to Raleigh together, but once there, they did not like the area.

After they decided to stay in Rochester, Tim took a job

Tim and Christine, so in love, visited Tim's sister Marilee in sunny Florida during their courtship. (Courtesy of Timothy D. Wells)

as a systems analyst at a small software firm called Phoenix. They created software for telecom companies. He worked there less than a year. He missed the teaching he had done at Yourdon, and he approached the University of Rochester and RIT business schools about teaching as an adjunct. RIT's business school forwarded his inquiry to the new department of information technology. Tim interviewed with Jeff Lasky, who hired him to teach an evening course on systems analysis. His initial student evaluations were great.

The next trimester, Lasky told Tim of an opening and asked if he would be interested in joining the department full time. At that time, RIT did not require a Ph.D. for tenure-track positions as long as the applicant had significant business experience. Tim met with the faculty and gave a colloquium. A few days later, he received a call offering him a position as an

assistant professor for the coming fall trimester. Tim really liked this idea.

On May 19, 1990, two years after Tim Wells and Christine Sevilla met, and a month after her divorce was finalized, they were married in their new church, the First Unitarian Church of Rochester, by the Reverend Richard Gilbert. Everyone who attended could see they were very

This wedding portrait of Tim and Christine was taken at the camera shop where Christine once worked. On her wedding day, Christine was an elegant and beautiful bride. She anticipated marrying a man who worshiped her. (Courtesy of Timothy D. Wells)

much in love. Years later, Scott Tayler, another First Unitarian Church minister, remembered, "The congregation was very close, very close not only to Tim and Christine but to the marriage of Tim and Christine."

One of the people most heartened by the wedding was Christine's old friend Ernie Lederman. He had long known "how guileless she was—honest to the depths of that soul," he said. "I was there through her painful illnesses, her tribulations with the men in her life, her toil at jobs she didn't always like, her bafflement at the lengths to which some people will go in order to get some money or some small political advantage."

She was plenty independent, Ernie felt. "She didn't ask for tangible help; emotional support was what she wanted and needed. I was as happy as a friend could be when she married Tim. At last, she had found the love she had sought: a man who could 'get' her, a companion, a foil for her emotionalism, an artistic peer, someone she could give to. I think it was the lack of a man who could receive and appreciate her gifts of love that had been the most painful of her trials. She flourished, artistically and emotionally, with Tim and wound up a leader in the causes that mattered most to her."

Ernie understood why they were attracted as a couple. He described Christine as "passionate, even obsessive about her causes." Tim, on the other hand, was so easygoing. Ernie even referred to him as "Señor Angel."

Christine's first husband approved. Paul Malatesta, who had stayed in touch with her through the years, thought she was very happy with her new partner.

Not long after the wedding, Christine and Tim bought an airy two-bedroom ranch in Pittsford. "We actually looked only at ranch houses because Amanda, Christine's dog, was getting old and arthritic," Tim recalled. The white house was set on an acre of land, with trees and a backyard that sloped down to a wooded stream. Its size was perfect for a childless couple. In time, the living room would become the heart of their home. Laid with a beige carpet, the long room was light and airy. With many musical instruments resting on their stands, the room would pronounce their mutual love of making music. Photographs covered much of the available wall space of the master bedroom. Adjacent to it was Tim's home office, a suitably messy professor's affair. The wall was lined with books and a profusion of tangled computer paraphernalia.

All was not bliss for the newlyweds, however. Tim recalled, "The weeks after we purchased the house were a real strain. We were trying to get the house in shape—painting, pulling up carpet, lawn work. Every appliance broke down. Everything was more expensive than we'd planned. Everything took longer than we expected. We were tired, sore, and angry. Each of us was saying, 'I only agreed to buy this house because you wanted it.' We were exhausted and both crying. I was also starting my new job at RIT." When asked, Tim denied they had any overt arguments. They got through this difficult time by deciding to get away for a few days. Finding a bed and breakfast down in the Finger Lakes that allowed dogs, they left their home improvements unfinished and agreed that fixing the house would be a long-term project.

Tim said that, in general, when he and Christine disagreed on a subject, they'd go silent rather than talk out their differences. They would essentially bury the issue and avoid confrontation, then move on to a new, more pleasant topic. He characterized this as an "avoidance dance." They learned to avoid unpleasantries.

One issue they did agree on was not having children. Christine had previously told Tim about her hysterectomy, and he had long before had a vasectomy. They did talk some about adoption, but that didn't go very far. "It scared her and didn't set well with me, either," he commented. They were both approaching forty. "We were comfortable and doubted we could—or would want to—adjust to the rigors and responsibilities of parenting."

Besides, they were dog people, which meant that their dogs were their children. For several more years they cared for Christine's aging dog, Amanda. When she passed away, their grief was profound. It wasn't until 1995 that they were prepared to welcome a new dog into their home. Anna Riley, a springer spaniel, was purchased before she was born. Tim and Christine attended a number of dog shows and found a breeder near Buffalo. When the litter was born, the breeder named the puppies alphabetically in birth order (Anna, Bailey, Carter, Diana, and so on). They picked the best, show-quality dogs to keep and sold the others. Tim and Christine went to see the litter when the puppies were a month old, and they both noticed Anna. "She was the most active and seemed to have a personality we both liked. We picked her up at nine weeks," Tim recalled. Yet during the first few weeks, they realized that she was not an "Anna" personality. To them, the name connoted a demure dog. Their new puppy was willful, assertive, and demanding. Christine liked the name Riley in general, and it seemed to fit, so they registered her as Anna Riley.

Their married life settled into a routine they both enjoyed. Tim generally arose at six thirty. He would let Riley out and feed her. He would make coffee and toast, which he served to Christine in bed. While eating, they would listen to NPR together before getting dressed. Four mornings per week, the couple would exercise together at the YMCA for forty-five minutes and then return home by nine. Two days per week, Tim had teaching responsibilities and departed for RIT by nine thirty. Classes typically lasted two hours, and after class, Tim worked in his campus office until two thirty or three.

On his way home he would buy food, because he had found out early in their marriage that Christine did not like grocery shopping. Tim usually prepared their dinner, and they regularly ate together around eight o'clock, often watching television and chatting. After dinner, they might work on their choral parts for the following Sunday before working separately. They would watch the "Late Show with David Letterman" together, after which Tim usually went to bed. Christine would often work until two or three in the morning.

While the two did not socialize often, Christine was more outgoing than her introverted husband. "I never went to anything on my own other than faculty meetings. I relied on her for all the social things," Tim said. "I had colleagues at RIT, but I did not work to create friendships. They were high maintenance. I felt awkward about the vulnerability it required." He was lucky that Christine would shoo him out the door. Otherwise, he likely would have stayed at home.

Although they did not socialize with people from the church, it remained the center of their outside activities. "The First Unitarian Church was very important to us," Tim noted. "We sang in the choir for twenty years. We occasionally served on committees and often helped with fundraising events. We helped with summer services. We provided a number of services and often wrote and performed music. Christine was chair of the arts committee for many years."

After leaving their choir, the two joined the Madrigalia. They also took their twinned voices to local coffeehouses, music festivals, and parties. Tim continued to play guitar, but he also learned the bass to back up his wife. When she took an interest in music from Spain, he learned to sing in Spanish, friends said. Like the roles they played in their marriage, their singing partnerships starred Christine. Choir member Grace Carswell told the local paper, "Christine sang more solos, though that doesn't necessarily mean she had the better voice." By her force of character, Christine grabbed the spotlight.

They did not entertain regularly, but for a number of years they hosted an annual Yankee Auction during the holidays where church friends would gather for an evening of caroling and exchanging casual gifts. During the early and middle years of their marriage, Christine invited friends involved with music for an evening of singing several times a year. They also attended each other's events. Tim had periodic faculty functions, and Christine had circles of friends—many from before they met—who would occasionally throw parties.

The couple also socialized with their neighbors. One of them, Janet Yaeger, thought they had a perfect marriage. "There are many people who would love to have the relationship they had," she commented. Two neighbors whom they particularly liked were Don and Paula Bataille. Paula had a special-education and fine-arts background, which led to discussions with Christine. The two couples also watched each other's homes when one was away. Every few months they chatted at the edge of their lawns and would discover that between the contents of their refrigerators they had a complete meal. "We'd get together at one of our homes around eight o'clock and fix dinner," Tim remembered. "Then we'd watch a movie or, more often, just talk."

As a person who came to know the couple well, Paula felt that Christine and Tim were a very caring couple. They held hands in public. Paula never witnessed an overt fight between the couple over the many years she knew them. She always found Tim in particular "a wonderful person, kind, gentle . . .

scholarly . . . musical . . . very loving with his family and friends
and neighbors." At the same time, however, she was critical
of their unequal partnership. She termed their relationship
"very codependent," with Tim taking care of Christine's
"narcissism." She had a very "high, shrill voice" and would
often yell for her husband to come help her out. Whenever
they got together, Tim "had to do a recitation of Christine's
accomplishments." In addition, Paula said that when Tim did
the cooking, Christine was allowed to present the meal as if
she had prepared it. When asked if this was true, he replied,
"Christine did not take credit for the things I did."

As a couple, Tim and Christine went out more frequently
than they entertained. Once a month, Christine would want
to see some art opening or museum event. She would ask
if he wanted come with her. Usually he did, but sometimes
he would say it didn't sound interesting, but she should go
by herself. She would frown and respond, "No, we can stay
home." Eventually, he would come around and say he'd be
happy to go with her.

Early on, Tim gave up the one social activity he enjoyed,
acting in plays—because Christine didn't approve. While
they were still dating, she gamely came with her best friend,
Beverly, to see Tim in a play, but she didn't say anything about
it afterward. Tim didn't notice her disapproval that time, but
in the first year they were married, when he played Sir Edward,
a small part in *The King and I*, with the Pittsford Musical Group,
Christine expressed displeasure with the rehearsal schedule,
because they took up so many evenings. He found out later,
when he saw that a road show for the *Phantom of the Opera*
was coming to Rochester, that she really didn't like musicals
at all. Prior to his sentencing, Tim acknowledged in his diary
his perplexity over this: "It was such a strange thing because
looking back, I really enjoyed the theater." In what was a well-

worn pattern by now, he sacrificed his passions to make his wife happy.

Christine's own passion was photography. That's why she connected with Dr. Dan Neuberger, a Rochester photographer and artist. They met through a weekly artists' breakfast group that Dan had started in 1989 with a few other artists. Dan described Christine as very creative, very talented, and very intelligent. He had been the first Rochester photographer asked to join the Arena Art Group, a local organization founded in 1951 that promoted all types of art shows. Dan later sponsored Christine for this group, and she was approved for membership.

Once they became friendly, he had dinner at Tim and Christine's home several times. Dan noticed that she displayed "a very strong-willed personality" while Tim was "a very sweet and gentle man." He did feel that Tim was "henpecked." Like many others, he sensed that Christine "ran the show while Tim went along with it."

Unfortunately, her strong opinions about photography soon led to artistic differences. She felt that the artists' breakfast group was not sufficiently serious or organized. Several people left the group because Christine was so vocal in her opinions. On one occasion, Dan sponsored a very confident sculptress and painter for membership in the Arena Art Group, but Christine "torpedoed" this candidate, claiming that the woman was "unprofessional." Dan observed, "Christine got a bug up her ass." He subsequently sent her an e-mail, reproaching her for her opposition and inviting Christine to discuss it further with him. In her e-mail reply, she stated that they had "nothing to talk about."

This marked the end of their relationship. If they encountered each other at professional functions, Christine ignored him. Tim, however, continued to talk to Dan, as nice as ever. "She was fragile and insecure," Tim noted. "She would sometimes get sad. When I'd ask what was wrong, she'd lament that nobody liked her. I'd remind her of everyone who loved her, and she'd smile." After this, Tim was cast in the role of conciliator for his temperamental wife and her tempestuous relationships with others.

Tim was employed as an associate professor in information technology at RIT, and he worked there for nearly twenty years. His primary area was the online teaching of graduate students. Tim's office was located on the second floor in the Computer Information and Sciences building, room 2716. He was never a fan of the campus architecture, which many observers have likened to a prison. Tim's impression started the first time he went to the campus: "The monotonous brick and sharp edges provide no relief for the eye, creating a sense of harshness and anxiety. The pattern used for entrances made me feel that I was always using the back door." Tim's dislike of the architecture, however, did not interfere with his early success. "I was one of the top-rated online instructors," he noted proudly.

Tim was instrumental in helping Christine take the next step forward in her career. She decided to enroll in the instructional design master's program in the human resource development department at RIT. She got a tuition waiver because Tim was on faculty. "She used her course projects to help staff at Strong," Tim related, "but she said she got resistance all the time."

The couple wrote a paper together that led to their attending a conference in Portugal in 1995. This was one of Tim's favorite memories of the marriage. They followed up that trip to the Iberian Peninsula with another to Spain the next year. This time it was a trip with all of the Sevilla siblings. Christine spent a great deal of time reestablishing

Tim and Christine enjoyed a folk-singing festival where they sang as a duo. Tim wore a Sevilla T-shirt that he had purchased for his wife on a trip to Spain. (Courtesy of Timothy D. Wells)

connections to family in Spain, because both sets of grandparents had emigrated from there. "The six of us—her two brothers and spouses and I—went to Spain the first time," Tim remembered. "It was great fun and rewarding for all of us."

Christine later penned her self-published *Memorias—An American in Spain, a Spaniard in America.* She wrote about how important it was for her to connect with her relatives in Spain and learn about her family history. Christine recalled, "I stayed long enough to enter their everyday lives and long enough to know the link of my past with their present."

This first, short visit reawakened Christine's artistic sensibilities, and she decided to make a return trip the next year to shoot a series of photos of her family, which would also be included in *Memorias.* Yet Tim did not enjoy this trip as much. "She went back and spent a month there in Spain initially without me because I had to teach courses. But then I went over and met her and it was very strange, just finding her in Spain." This time he was excluded from the family bonding. "That whole trip, I felt kind of out of place."

Despite feeling removed, he strongly supported Christine's next move. After years of being unhappy at Strong Memorial Hospital, she quit her job in 1995. Part of the reason was because she and Tim planned to start a new business enterprise. In 1997, a year after she earned her master's degree in instructional technology from RIT, and Tim was awarded tenure, she founded her own company, Lumin Guild. She was president and Tim was vice president. Tim said he preferred being "second in command." She earned $600 a month, which was paid into a retirement account. Lumin Guild was an instructional design firm, meaning that it created instructional material and job and training aids and designed brochures.

Like many fledgling operations, Lumin Guild depended at first on personal contacts for its business. Christine secured a contract with RIT to create three online courses. RIT liked the services she provided, and in 2000 they hired her as an adjunct professor to teach the classes she had created for the master's-level human resource development program. She also assisted Tim's sister Marilee with the logistics of her midwife practice, and she helped a friend, Dr. Ninke Dosa, to create a Web site on adolescents with spina bifida.

Trying to spread their wings, Christine and Tim subcontracted with other companies to build more user-friendly training materials for auto and insurance companies. The impatience that Christine had shown while working at Strong Memorial Hospital, though, would hurt their new business. Tim shared, "As a friend she was delightful. As a business associate she was frustrating. In the early years of Lumin Guild she tried to form alliances with people who were better at marketing than we were. She would subcontract on training-development projects but was frustrated by the prime contractor overcommitting or promising work that she didn't feel was the right solution."

For several years, their company attracted high-profile corporate and nonprofit clients and made modest profits. In 2002, they coauthored the humorously titled digital article "Where the Wired Things Are" and, a year later, a book called *Maximizing the Enterprise Information Assets*, published by Auerbach Press.

By that time, however, Tim had had his name removed from the corporate listing, and the Lumin Guild Web site started to become a more private endeavor, serving as a vehicle for Christine's artistic efforts. All along, her vision of Lumin Guild was a guild-like environment where friends and people she liked working with got together to collaborate on interesting and useful projects. As time passed, she concentrated more on expressing her concerns about the environment through art and photography, working with the Cornell University Cooperative Extension and the Black Creek Watershed preservations. "Sometimes these efforts were supported by grant money," Tim related, "but more often they were just projects she wanted to do." To please Christine, Tim provided the working capital for these projects.

One anchor of the Lumin Guild Web site was a series of applications using a secure online conferencing system that Tim had previously developed. He named this Colloquy, another word for a formal, usually written discussion. While this definition appealed to Tim cerebrally, more importantly he loved the way it felt on his lips. Colloquy was supposed to support online learning, team collaboration, and media research. His original intent was to promote better instruction with Colloquy because he never liked the other commercial systems supporting online learning. He thought his program provided a better dialogue feature and was more suited for curriculum refinement and shared material.

In its early development, Tim used Colloquy for all of his online classes starting in 1996 and lasting ten years. In fact, he tried to convince RIT to use it as a base for all their online learning. Yet the office of online learning decided it was more prudent to use a standard commercial package. Tim kept working on and using Colloquy in his classes until the department strongly suggested they wanted all courses to use the same program. "Colloquy was my great hope and my great disappointment," Tim said. "It had been my mythical golden apple and my huge stumbling block." Tim remembered his work on Colloquy as "an endless cycle of hope and failure," a sentiment that described the recurring disappointments throughout his career.

Stymied in the office of online learning, Tim joined a group
of faculty and research at the National Technical Institute
for the Deaf, a school at RIT, in a grant-funded project with
the goal of using Colloquy to allow faculty in Denmark and
Rochester to build a curriculum for deaf students using
shared material and evaluations of the outcomes. "It paid
for a nice trip to Denmark," Tim noted, and Christine came
along. Later, however, the project team also decided to use a
commercial package.

Tim would not give up his dream. In the late 1990s, he
accepted the position of director of multidisciplinary studies
with the hope of using Colloquy to coordinate curriculum
development, faculty dialogue, and class sessions across
a network of international colleges and universities. He
worked with Wiley McKinzie, an RIT dean and, at one time,
Tim's boss, to develop programs for students to study abroad.
Tim recalled, "Rather than teaching, I'd be coordinating
the shared development of a dynamic curriculum. The
Colloquy would allow both sharing of material and
monitoring of student progress in different institutions.
This effort included several trips—Japan, India, Taiwan. We
paid for Christine to come with me." In the end, though,
he failed to get Colloquy and arrangements in place. These
programs proved to be unsuccessful, with the exception of
the one in Taiwan, and even that program ultimately folded
due to government regulations. As a consequence, Tim was
returned to a faculty position.

A telling incident occurred during the course of their
international travel, one that was emblematic of Tim's
tendency to put on a good face for his coworkers. He brought
Christine along to India on one of their trips. Wiley recalled
that after a long day of negotiations, Tim invited Christine
to join them for dinner. "Christine immediately tore into

Tim about having to sit in the hotel. She was merciless and would not let up." He knew that Tim was not open about his feelings, but this barrage took Wiley by surprise. Wiley said this was one of the most embarrassing things he had ever seen. He felt an urge to get up and leave the table, describing the onslaught as "very humiliating." After this dinner, he avoided meeting with them again as a couple for the remainder of the trip.

Wiley was also perplexed that Tim never attempted to discuss that ill-fated dinner later. For Tim, it never happened. When he was asked about the dinner after the murder, his recollection was entirely different. He acknowledged that Christine had a temper with others, but he claimed she shielded him from these outbursts. Tim felt that his role in their marriage was to "calm her down." He reveled in the thought that she needed him. Tim assumed the role of central supporter, conceding to and accommodating her needs while submerging and subordinating his own. For Tim, the unspoken bargain of mortgaging his own needs to gain Christine's acceptance was worth any cost, even if in the end this meant the roles he accepted would take him far away from his authentic self.

Tim had no idea how much he would later regret his constant denial of his own desires. He enjoyed hearing Christine say to him, "You are really the only person who would put up with me." In the end, though, his dependence on fulfilling her needs would have disastrous consequences.

CHAPTER 6

CROSSING STARS

Christine Sevilla's freedom from a nine-to-five job led to her blossoming during the second decade of her marriage to Tim Wells. She built on her love of nature photography to become an impassioned advocate for the environment. Her husband, however, had already reached the zenith of his career. He had been trying to keep up with the rapidly changing field of information technology, but as the years passed, he fell further and further behind. While Christine became a leader, Tim came to call himself a fraud.

At first the nature of their marriage didn't seem to change. Tim and Christine still socialized as they always had, with church and music the center of their activities. Their comfortable world began breaking up when the Reverend Richard Gilbert decided to retire in 2002, after thirty-two years leading the Unitarian Church. For the following two years, the church had only interim ministers, until Kaaren Anderson and Scott Tayler were hired as parish co-ministers.

That did not sit well with Christine, and therefore with Tim. When the selection committee proposed the new ministers, they cast the only dissenting votes. They felt that the new ministers were too self-centered. As the first year passed, Christine and Tim were both troubled by the changes being made. They thought the church was supposed to support individual members to do good things. Scott and Kaaren seemed to implement a ministry where the members' roles were to support the church and aggrandize the ministers in the process. Most of the congregation was willing to go along with the changes, but Tim wanted to leave, as did some other members. He began referring to himself as an atheist.

Christine wanted to stay and fight. She helped form a small group who called themselves the Concerned Congregants. Their goal was to question the direction of the church. The ministers turned away two attempts to start discussion groups. The group managed to call a special meeting of the congregation, but it didn't go anywhere. Frustrated by being on the outside of governance, Christine and Tim ran for the Board of Trustees. They were not elected under "very suspicious circumstances," Tim believed. He said to Christine that he didn't see how their protest efforts would succeed and it was only causing them angst. She would agree with Tim but then set up another meeting of the Concerned Congregants. Being his agreeable self, he went with her and helped as he could.

Tim, who always hated confrontations, sought another way out. In 2006, they left their church choir but soon missed it. The next year, Tim saw a new possibility. He read that the Madrigalia Chamber Singers, a local singing group, was holding auditions. According to Paula Bataille, Tim was accepted, but Christine was not. He insisted, however, that they be admitted as a pair, and so they were. Tim had an ulterior purpose in mind. He wanted to get Christine away from the Concerned Congregants.

They both loved singing in Madrigalia. The music was complex, challenging, and beautiful when it came together. Tim became a member of the board and was slated to become their treasurer in 2010. Christine immersed herself in promotions, communication, and the design of the programs. She also worked with other members deciding on new costumes for their concerts.

As time went on, Tim and Christine formed an informal band with RIT coworkers Jorge Díaz-Herrera, a dean of the college, and Carl Atkins, director of the music department. They called their group Sun de la Terra, loosely translated to mean "sun of the earth." They occasionally gathered with mutual friends for an evening of music and socializing.

The group also performed together. One of their more noteworthy gigs was a concert at Harmony House in 2009. Heartland Concerts also offered them a slot in their annual folk-music series. Ever the imaginative artist, Christine designed a striking promotional photo of the two of them with their heads side by side but placed in opposite directions. It was a challenge for Tim to depress the camera's shutter release while also preserving the unique positions they assumed for the photo. Heartland Concerts used the image, with Christine shown upside down, to market their upcoming performance. Sun de le Terra performed several South American songs that day. "It was great fun," Tim recalled, "and Christine put a lot of effort into getting friends involved." Tim and Christine performed a duet, and she invited friends from their church to do a series of a cappella songs.

Their chosen music stemmed from Christine's interest in Spanish music, reflecting her family heritage. That she was supposed to be the star of the show was not in doubt. A close colleague of Tim's attended their concerts because she too was friends with Jorge Díaz-Herrera. She had also known Tim ever since he joined the faculty. She did not think Tim and Christine made sweet harmony. She described Christine as a very impatient person who reacted to frustration with an edgy intensity. She stated, "I felt sorry for Tim, who I knew as a kind individual. I was sorry he would be subjected to this." Her intuition was that Christine was verbally abusive to Tim, although she never saw them fight.

Tim didn't mind, though. He was glad to play second fiddle. "In most of our singing, I was the one supporting her. I was the one who did the harmonies," he said. He was so practiced in this role that he put aside the fact that he had the technical vocal training and, by most accounts, the better voice.

On two occasions, Christine was away when the couple was

asked to perform. Tim thought he couldn't go on without her, but in both cases the audience reacted very positively. "I had done coffeehouses and performances all my life. It wasn't so much a lack of confidence. It just felt so strange to be singing without her, but then to have the audience respond so well was nice, actually." Once while she was in Spain, Tim attended an open-microphone performance at a club on Gregory Street. He and Christine had gone there occasionally to spend an evening and sing. That evening he introduced James Taylor's "Mill Worker" and said he had always thought it was a beautiful song about being trapped in a job. He commented to the audience that his wife didn't like this song because she felt that the singer is apologizing. Somebody in the audience shouted out, "Well, she's not here!" Tim knew the song very well, and when he sang it, he received a great response from the audience.

He created the same enthusiasm on another occasion when the two were scheduled to sing for the Turtle Hill Folk Festival, an annual event held by the local Golden Link Folk Singing Society. During the day they scheduled local artists to perform, and one session focused on ballads. The organizers had asked Tim and Christine to take that slot, but Christine couldn't make it and Tim couldn't say no. "I remember my aunt Ruth was coming through at that same time. She came straight to the Turtle Hill Folk Festival and listened to my little set. It felt good, too."

Still, these were only isolated occasions. Tim much preferred to ride on Christine's coattails. As he pointed out, "She loved putting projects together and bringing others in." A shining example was the Springing Green Madrigalia concert. This was Christine's brainchild, held over three days in May 2009. She joined her passions for music and the environment to convince Madrigalia to expand its annual spring concert to celebrate nature. She enlisted a wide range of environmental organizations as cosponsors of the event.

By this time, Christine's newly developed love for protecting the environment was in full swing. She had been taking photographs for years, and she increasingly focused on images of flowers. These photographs were displayed in a City Hall gallery. Her brother Michael commented, "Her early work in the camera store was a perfect start to her interest in photography. As we know, she became a fantastic nature photographer."

Christine's friend Steven believed that focusing on flowers led to other plants, and that led to a broader environmental awareness. "Looking at her photography, you could really see an evolution from pretty pictures of flowers in the eighties and the nineties to . . . her really looking more at the bigger picture—looking at weeds from an artistic standpoint and in terms of their place in the ecosystem," he said.

Over a five-year period, Christine published, at Lumin Guild's expense, a series of small books of photographs and prose about nature, particularly wetlands. She slogged into swamps and led hikes to search for invasive plants. "She was a very elegant woman," said Steven. "She didn't give the impression of a rugged outdoors person. But she was tough." Her brother Michael heartily concurred. "With friends interested in preserving the environment, her passion for protecting the wetlands blossomed, an interest she captured magnificently in her photographs, maps, calendars, and books."

Like any dedicated camera buff, Christine had a variety of cameras. The two she used most often were a Canon through-the-lens digital and a Canon pocket-sized digital, Tim recalled. For her film photography, she mainly used an Olympus.

As Tim's interest in teaching declined, he increasingly joined her on her many trips to photograph specimens in the area's parks. He lugged her camera equipment, and she laughingly called him her Sherpa, referring to the local porters for mountaineers in the Himalayas. Tim wistfully recalled, "She took a photo I love of me with a bag over one shoulder, a tripod on the other. I was looking down at Riley, who was sitting next to me, looking up with this big smile on her face. I really liked getting out with Riley and Christine."

While Tim didn't mind taking a backseat in their vocal performances, he did feel ignored at the photography events they attended. "I often felt a little slighted, because I had helped her prepare the matting and mounting for various pieces," he said. "Some of them were very interesting." Christine became a regular participant at an annual photography competition called Statewide Lakeside at the Oswego Civic Arts Center. She did very well there, and one time she won the Patron's Choice award. "She'd get this little girlish look," Tim wistfully recalled. "She was always a very mature looking woman, but at those moments when she was getting some attention, you would see this childlike look of anticipation." When it came time for the awards to be announced, she would edge away from Tim. She wanted to be all alone if her name was called. This habit was not so endearing to Tim. "It bothered me a lot," he recalled. "I didn't say anything, but my feelings were hurt. I really didn't understand why she would move away from me."

Whatever Christine's reasons for this, there was no doubt that she was becoming well known for her work. As she gained a reputation, her artistic efforts began to extend far beyond individual photographs. With so much natural bounty to highlight, she expanded into creating brochures and booklets.

Her environmental work encompassed a range of topics. Christine wrote, published, and distributed *A Guide to Public Access Wetlands In and Near Monroe County*. This was one of her most extensive projects. In 2004, the Environmental Protection Agency awarded her a Wetland Protection

Project Grant of $30,000 to help her realize her vision. She also developed and published the accompanying book, *Creating a Wetland Guidebook: A Tutorial.* Both manuals were designed to educate a broad audience about fragile wetland environments. Partners that Christine enlisted to help with this project included the Nature Conservancy, the Genesee Land Trust, the Genesee Valley Audubon Society, as well as other environmental organizations.

"Garden Villains: Invasive Plants and Tree Species, Monroe County" was a brochure that Christine began in 2006. She cobbled together funding from various environmental groups for a first printing, and the New York State Department of Environmental Conservation financed a second printing of 10,000 copies.

"Weed-Suppressive Groundcovers" was a pamphlet Christine developed with Cornell University Cooperative Extension, among others. It was designed to educate homeowners and landscapers that the fewer weeds in a landscape, the less herbicide had to be used.

"In Abeyance: Hemlock and Canadice," a self-published catalog of an exhibit Christine presented in 2007, was intended to motivate long-term preservation of Hemlock and Canadice lakes, two of the westernmost, smaller of New York's Finger Lakes, located south of Rochester. In this case, her efforts helped to build the political momentum that resulted in the creation of the Hemlock-Canadice State Forest.

In 2009, Christine never traveled without "The Black Creek Watershed: Map Guide," a pamphlet and map she designed. She gave her work out at public meetings, social occasions, church gatherings, and group hikes.

Nature lovers all across the region greatly appreciated Christine's wide-ranging efforts. As time went on, she became more and more committed to the cause. Like many environmentalists, she embraced the call to educate others, even if that led to confrontations.

One of her neighbors, Patricia Knoll, knew how strongly Christine felt about the parks in the area, especially Mendon Ponds County Park. She said that Christine visited the park frequently and had a habit of confronting mountain bikers illegally riding on its trails. She would go so far as to take photographs of these riders and their license plates, threatening to turn them in to the authorities for damaging the environment.

Sara Rubin, another friend of Christine's, worked with her on the local Sierra Club chapter's wetlands committee. She recognized Christine's "sense of justice—her energy and honesty." Sara told the *Democrat and Chronicle*, "She just wouldn't let anything go. She confronted various public officials."

Christine's environmental activism took on a special focus when she helped Nora Bredes, the founding executive director of the New York League of Conservation Voters, campaign for a seat in the county legislature in 2009. Nora described her as "intelligent, inspired, beautiful, caring, and fierce." They had first met at the First Unitarian Church when Nora and her family moved to Rochester ten years prior. They saw each other at various church functions, but they didn't get well acquainted until they began to work together on environmental issues during the campaign. "Working to preserve fragile parklands from inappropriate use and political opportunism, we established a close, inspiring working partnership," Nora stated. "Christine became one of my genuine friends."

Christine also became friends with Kimberly Hartquist. They met after Christine spoke out at a town meeting against the county's new master plan for its parks. "Her eyes sparkled with such genuine passion and drive that one could not help but join her cause," Kimberly remembered. For most of the following year, they shared many e-mails about their work. "Her wry sense of humor mixed with her passionate drive inspired me to do things I had never done, such as speak at county legislator meetings. Christine was pretty shy about speaking in front of groups, but she always did anyway—because she had to. If she could, then so could I."

Christine persuaded Kimberly to help campaign for Nora Bredes. She was determined to knock on every door in her section of the electoral district. Yet Christine had no desire to run for any type of office herself. "At one point, I called her a leader," Kimberly recalled, "and she instantly rebelled from this title. Yet she had already rallied a number of environmentalists into a group she called Parks Preservation." The group coordinated efforts to keep an eye on the county's master-plan process.

As active as Christine became, she did not neglect her family. Although her parents still resided in California and her brothers lived in San Diego and Michigan, she used e-mail to keep in touch. Her brother Chuck commented, "To our immediate family, Christine was the glue who kept us closer together. We were connected to her by almost daily e-mails on diverse topics: environmental, political, and personal. Those contacts made it seem like we were engaged in an almost daily dialogue with her. Christine was the one who maintained the contacts with our extended family—the many cousins, aunts, and uncles who are scattered about the country." Christine and Chuck also discussed projects they were working on, becoming closer through their shared interests. He would send his sister an occasional poem or political lyrics for a new tune, which she would always tell him were wonderful. Chuck noted, "For years the walls of my office at work have been filled with her artwork, as they were beautiful and kept us closer."

Touchingly, Christine reached out to her ninety-year-old father on several of her projects. In his retirement, he had taken up painting, and as a gift to him on his birthday in 2008, she made business cards that featured his work. Together they created a calendar with his art and her photographs. This project provided her father with an outlet for his talents and gave both of them the joy of collaborating together.

Despite the filial warmth, Christine's choice of title for the calendar was quite dark. It was "Thanatopsis," taken from a poem by nineteenth-century American poet William Cullen Bryant. The title is loosely translated from Greek to mean "meditation upon death." Tim remarked that Christine was captivated by the idea. "She used it as a title for three collections. She did a collection of images of big-box stores and another of a group of nice little houses in Greece that were being torn down to make way for a Walmart superstore." In terms of the calendar's theme, he noted, "She was very concerned about invasive plants. She did this series to highlight how beautiful the plants can be and still be so damaging, and how humans can be duped by some allure while being part of our own destruction." When asked if her calendar's subject was in response to his worsening depression, he replied, "The timing is ironic. I don't know if she sensed something. Her yearly calendars always reflected what she was working on at the time." Her final work, this meditation on death, was released just weeks before her murder.

Christine Sevilla had come into her own. She was doing what she loved, and she loved being recognized for her contributions, whether in photography, environmental affairs, or music. She was blossoming as she reached her late fifties. Yet somehow she did not notice that the rising of her star was being accompanied by the falling of Tim's. Love is not necessarily a zero-sum game, in which what is gained by one is taken from the other, but that's the way it was working out in the Wells household.

In this light, an observation made by their neighbor, Paula

THANATOPSIS:

2010 CALENDAR
More invasive plant species
of the Finger Lakes Region

Christine Sevilla
LUMIN GUILD

Shortly before her murder, Christine completed this 2010 calendar, using the eerie title "Thanatopsis" (meaning "meditation upon death"). Her calendar highlighted how something that appears beautiful can actually be damaging. (Courtesy of Timothy D. Wells)

Bataille, is striking. Paula recalled that about three years before the murder, Christine became "smothering" with her. She clarified this by explaining that Christine "had to crawl into somebody else's skin and would usurp the energy from them." Christine's relationship with Paula became so close that she even began referring to her as "Mom." Over the years of their relationship, Paula came to believe that had "schizophrenic tendencies." This belief was bolstered by Christine's admission that her mother suffered from schizophrenia. At one point Paula shared her concerns with Tim, insisting that Christine had a mental disorder. Predictably, Tim promptly dismissed her concerns.

According to Paula, Christine's longing for recognition was relentless. She told people she was a member of Mensa, a society whose members have highly superior IQs, and described herself as brilliant. She constantly demanded to be center stage and required continuous validation. Paula saw the same dynamic between husband and wife. When asked if Christine was good to Tim, she replied, "No, I felt she was there to be served." She said a more apt term for her was "Princess Christine." In this regard, Paula claimed that Christine took exclusive credit for achievements, even if they were largely facilitated or accomplished by Tim. "Tim was like her lap dog," she said. "He'd ask, 'How high?'"

Christine's sister-in-law Donna Sevilla had a different view of the unfolding tragedy. She credited Tim with "supporting and nurturing her gifts." She continued, "In the early years, he appeared to mentor her musical talent and supported her art with the technical skills necessary to produce and publish her beautiful photography. He had a background of musical training and he certainly had the technical skills." Donna concluded that he was "comfortable in the role of mentor and felt diminished and unable to accept the role of equal."

It may well be that Christine was unaware of Tim's decline, because it happened so gradually. They had grown comfortable in their marriage. He recalled, "We were together in the same space. I would make it a point to get home as often as I could to be her Sherpa. I found that a nice escape. I could rationalize not being at RIT." Nor should it be forgotten what a good actor Tim was. She did not see his growing list of failures because he hid them so skillfully from her.

They had grown distant in one key regard—their sexual relationship, or lack of one. Tim said that he had never cared that much about sex with her anyway. Their lovemaking was "nothing terribly passionate," he noted. "It was nothing acrobatic; it was very simple." Over the years, whatever physical interest they had in each other dwindled down to zero. Tim estimated that, by the time of the murder, they had not had sex in five years. He denied this was a source of any discomfort for them. Christine "seemed content to not have sex," he observed. "We never talked about it." However, it was apparent Tim had retained some libido, because he masturbated several times per month.

Such submissive behavior seemed odd for a man who had seven affairs during his first marriage. One commonality that tied the two marriages together was Tim's loss of sexual interest in both of his wives. He admitted, "With neither did I feel the longing and infatuation I felt with Patty in high school, nor the desire I felt for Terri and Lindsey, or the wondrous feeling that came with the thought of Terri being pregnant by me."

Tim and Christine did cuddle with each other when they slept, although, tellingly, he couldn't remember the last time that they had done even that. He was the one who initiated contact, rolling over and putting his arm around her. "I would give her a hug, and she would make this really, really wonderful female sound and a pleased appreciative smile. I loved that; it was such a pretty thing. I don't remember the last time she did that."

Part of the reason was Tim's longstanding discomfort with sexual relations. During one affair, Tim's lover told him that she chronically lied to her husband about enjoying sex. Ever since that time, Tim had suffered from a nagging doubt that the women he bedded did the same to him. He staunchly denied any infidelity during his marriage to Christine, nor did he believe Christine was ever unfaithful to him.

Given that Tim's interest in sex was waning, it was not surprising that his primary-care physician, Dr. Charlene Conners, advised him in July of 2009 that he had an abnormally low testosterone level. She provided him with a prescription for a testosterone supplement, but Tim was reluctant to fill it, citing the unlikely excuse that its cost prohibited him from taking it on a regular basis. In an attempt to encourage Tim to try it, Dr. Conners gave him a coupon for a free sample. Yet it remained in its wrapper. In truth, Tim's refusal sprung from a psychological allergy to the idea of taking a masculine-enhancing hormone. Taking testosterone would violate his view of himself as a gentleman's gentleman.

Scientists have linked low testosterone levels to depression in older men. There is no doubt that Tim had been exhibiting these signs in many avenues of his life for quite some time. In particular, it may have fed a vicious cycle in his work life. He was already worried that he was falling behind, and the more depressed he became, the less able he was to concentrate or keep up. This accelerating downward spiral was clearly evident in his later years of teaching. Tim eventually reached a nadir where he was barely engaged with his students at all.

His failure to get RIT to accept his Colloquy program signaled a larger problem that Tim increasingly faced. As he grew older, he found himself struggling more and more to keep current with the rapid advances being made in computers. The explosion of the World Wide Web sent the need for new software into overdrive. It is well known that computer programming is a young man's game, and Tim was not a spring chicken anymore.

Tim did not simply give up. While continuing to teach, he

spent five years earning a master's in communication and media technologies through RIT and was finally awarded the degree in 2007. He also enrolled in a Ph.D. program in media psychology in 2005 at Fielding Institute, an online graduate-degree program based in Santa Barbara, California. With this degree, Tim hoped to introduce courses dealing with the effects of information technology on people's ordinary lives.

All of these efforts could not mask, however, his growing unease. "I started the master's in communications program with great enthusiasm, but it was like pulling teeth for me to complete the thesis," he said. "I really had great hopes for the Ph.D. program, but then it all seemed so futile. I could feel my ability to remain current in competing technology was slipping. I was awarded tenure, but soon after, I began viewing it as golden handcuffs. Looking back, I can see that I shifted my thinking from trying to stay ahead to trying to hang on until I could retire."

At home, Tim sat in front of his computer and pretended to work on his assignments for Fielding or read students' papers. He observed, "I felt like I wasn't doing what I was supposed to be doing." Growing anxiety limited his thinking and concentration. Tim developed the irrational fear that his brain was deteriorating. This belief was fed by his seeming inability to learn new things or grasp the advancing technologies he was expected to teach. Tim felt unable to contribute to his Ph.D. program's online discussions because he couldn't remember the authors of the theories and research.

As early as 2004, Tim began experiencing intermittent feelings of worthlessness and guilt. He mused, "I felt depressed because I couldn't keep up. But looking back, I now think depression caused my mental dullness, not the other way around." This is when he started likening himself to an imposter, going through the everyday motions of life but in the end knowing he was a fraud. "I retreated into Christine, and Riley, and the house. They became my identity. I would make any excuse to be with Christine and Riley. I was hoping against hope that I could keep going until I could retire or win the lottery, or something."

In spite of his escalating difficulties, Tim continued volunteering to assist students. "It felt really good to have people look at me with, oh, he went the extra mile, he did this, he didn't complain, he stepped up when that class had to be taught." Yet though Tim took over that responsibility, the support he offered became increasingly ineffectual.

Tim's prospects appeared bright when the information technology department announced a new initiative in late 2005. Tim and a colleague of his, Michael Yacci, were to offer a new master's-degree program, starting in the spring 2006 trimester. They planned to address growing needs in the arena of online learning. Companies were spending billions of dollars annually to educate and train their employees. The new master's program would focus on the creation of learning experiences, performance support, and knowledge-management systems. Unlike similar courses at other universities, the degree would be taught completely online, using a variety of e-learning techniques and systems. It would also be offered part time, to accommodate the schedules of students already working.

Yacci said in RIT's announcement, "Graduates of the program will be able to design systems that improve human performance through networked multimedia environments." Tim added, "Students who successfully complete the degree will be poised for leadership positions in e-learning, knowledge management, educational multimedia, corporate training, and virtual universities."

Despite the initial fanfare, though, the new degree

program had trouble attracting students. The university did not do much to promote it, so public knowledge that it even existed remained low. To help solve that problem, Tim saw a new opportunity for his program. "Mike Yacci and I were not getting any marketing support for our new MS degree. In a meeting with the chairman, I suggested that we use Colloquy to support a research and marketing effort. We could do content analysis on job ads like those featured on Monster. com, recruiting people in 'Knowledge Management' and 'Performance Improvement.' We could look for trends and patterns. The findings would be sent to the advertising companies with the message: 'You can develop your own experts by sending your personnel through our online degree program.'"

Everyone said it sounded like a great idea. There was one hitch, though. Tim had to deliver on his promise. "I remember the horrible feeling I had after that meeting. I had done it again. I'm not going to be able to do this." He had dumped another assignment on his plate that he was not capable of doing. He had to work harder to stay in place.

In the end, he never would complete the enhancements to Colloquy to support this new research. Tim reflected, "Looking back, I had to somehow know that the program was doomed at that point." He wasn't going to be able to do the one thing that would increase enrollment. "But I could putz around and look busy. I could rationalize it by saying the new features could be used in future research projects at Fielding and beyond."

Another reverse occurred when he tried to use Colloquy for a grant-funded project in conjunction with his colleague Dr. Robert Teese, in the math and physics department. Colloquy would support lab teams as they collaborated in the writing of lab reports, and it would assist in evaluating quality.

Yet once again, when Tim was put on the spot to supervise this project, he couldn't deliver. "I failed to coordinate the student programmers. They were so smart and quick, I couldn't keep up with them and lead them in the direction I had envisioned."

All through this period, Tim kept trying. He remembered the mantra that continually ran through his head. "All I have to do is do more and this will be solved. All I have to do is to expand Colloquy and I will be able to get the promotions and I will get students into the program. All I have to do is more work in the Ph.D. program and that will be solved."

At the same time, a seismic shift in computer technology left Tim with a program that used an unsupported language and database. The department was moving to Adobe Flash and Oracle Database, so he tried to convert what he had done and develop what he was planning to a new environment. Conversions and updates were nothing new to Tim. He'd had to keep up with other developing technology. "But," as he recalled, "this change was really big and difficult. I never recovered. I was always playing catch-up."

He had devoted a tremendous amount of effort to Colloquy, a program that was destined for the dustbin of history. The more futile his efforts became, the more despondent Tim became about his ability to keep up with his other responsibilities. "I used the Colloquy development as an excuse—a shield and cover for my own failures. And to hide what I was not doing from Christine. I tried to tie everything I was doing into the same core system. Christine asked me to add features to the Lumin Guild Web site using Colloquy. I told her I could do that and I justified the time spent because it was augmenting the same program I wanted to use for RIT and Fielding."

When Tim looked back, he summarized his academic career as a series of disappointments. He said he came out of the chute quickly but then lost his edge. While he believed that many of his ideas were great, only a small minority agreed. Hence his projects often ended without the success or accolades he desired. Asked if this generated resentment, Tim replied that he felt worthless, not resentful. "I felt like, I've done all that you asked me to. It felt like I can't do any more, and you're asking me to do more."

The growing tide of despair colored everything he did. "I found it easy to not complete assignments," he said. "I found it convenient not to spend the necessary time, not to keep up with the changing field." That's why he gladly agreed to accompany Christine on her photo jaunts. It allowed him to escape the unbearable amount of pressure he was feeling because of his accumulating failures.

"Needs Improvement"

RIT was very slow at recognizing how Tim's teaching and service had declined, but the university was not as ignorant as he thought. His longtime colleague Professor McKinzie had a firsthand view of this situation. "Tim had gone downhill in his teaching. He was unresponsive to students. He also rarely attended departmental meetings."

Tim's performance ratings reflected this decline. Whereas in the 1990s his ratings were "excellent," by 2006 they were "satisfactory." The following year, he "met expectations." By the year of Christine's murder, his performance was a bleak "needs improvement."

That was also the year that a new chairman, Dr. Jim Leone, took over Tim's department. When the master's-degree program was evaluated, Leone found that the low enrollment did not justify its continuance. He summoned Tim to his office and very gently spoke of Tim's need to pay more attention to his students. Leone reminded Tim of his early days at RIT and how impressive he was at that time. Tim understood. "I'm sure he wanted to inspire me and tell me that he knew I could perform well and creatively, but I felt absolutely defeated."

And then the fated e-mail came from Jeffrey Lasky, suspending the program altogether. Lasky concluded his memo by expressing a "more personal" concern: "I recall the lengthy and agonizing process that you endured to secure the program's approval, and I am aware of your passion for the degree and its subject matter. So, as a colleague and friend, I share your disappointment and frustration. . . . I will send out the announcement about the program to the department on Tuesday. I wish such an announcement was not necessary."

Another stunning blow followed several days later. Tim's performance was rated as "satisfactory," but in a review of his teaching, Leone wrote, "The student evaluations are disappointing. While not as bad as last year, they still reflect the actions of an instructor who is not attentive. . . . Tim taught six distance courses to a total of nineteen students for the entire twelve months. One would think that with such a low head count, paying attention to the students and their needs would be a low-maintenance task."

Tim knew very well how dismal his student evaluations were. "I got to the point where I wasn't reading the reviews. I kept waiting for the department chair to say something, I remember thinking. And all he would say when occasionally we would meet alone was, 'Tim, you need to respond quicker to your students. You need to stay more in touch.' I knew I needed to do a lot more than that."

Tim was disgusted with himself. He grew to hate attending RIT commencement exercises because he did not feel he was worthy of students' appreciation.

If he had read some of the later evaluations, he might have become even more depressed. Here is a random sampling of the shocking comments his former students wrote about him:

> Timothy Wells' apathy towards teaching is obvious. This is the third time I've suffered through this neglect. I can read on my own. I don't need to pay thousands of dollars to be given reading assignments. There were no lessons. No guidance. Nothing. He posted reading assignments and disappeared. Reappearing in week five to give everyone a glowing progress report and has not been heard from since. Do you know where he is? Is he even real?

> He created his own software to conduct the course. This software is much worse. Plus, why make students learn another tool for no reason? He took a couple weeks to get the feel for it. Honestly, I think the professor spent more time writing Colloquy than he did "instructing" us. The little that he did do was always late. He hardly provided any feedback. If that's all it takes to be an RIT professor, then hire me.

> The professor did not interact with the class at all. He ignored the vast majority of the posts. I have numerous questions that remain unanswered today. This class was a total waste of time and I resent being forced to put up with and pay for it.

> I am extremely disappointed with the lack of instruction from the professor. . . . I feel that, in no way, did I get any significant value from the large dollar investment made in this course. What an extremely sad class. RIT should be ashamed of offering it and charging for it. Professor Wells had no interaction with class whatsoever. Disappointed and will not recommend.

Due to the tremendous stress he was feeling, Tim developed terrible problems with insomnia. Nearly every night he woke up feeling tense and anxious. To stave off his feelings of inadequacy and depression, he developed a nasty drinking habit. By now he was consuming three to four glasses of wine alone every night after dinner. Tim denied ever feeling particularly intoxicated, although he was concerned this level of consumption might be harmful. While the alcohol provided short-term relief, this ritual created a dangerous cycle of dependency that left Tim looking gray and worn down most of the time.

It also left him overtly short-tempered for the first time in his life. Tim displayed sudden outbursts of anger that took his nearest and dearest by surprise. On one occasion, Christine was trying to cancel a subscription by phone after receiving an errant bill. Her attempt led to the frustration many people feel with a phone representative, and finally Tim interrupted the call and swore at the clerk.

After he hung up, he remarked, "I guess I went over the top."

Christine replied, "Yes, you did."

Riley had a keen sense of the unspoken tension, and she became a barometer for the stress in the Wells household, developing the skin allergy for which her veterinarian prescribed the special duck diet. Tim recalled he was perplexed and anxious that after a year of this diet, nothing was working to improve her skin condition. Yet once he was incarcerated and a new owner took over Riley's care, her problem mysteriously cleared up on its own.

In December 2008, Tim and Christine gathered with his family for a Christmas get-together. Everyone expected Tim to be his usual pleasant self. Yet while the family was having a political discussion, Tim became visibly angry. His family noted his fists were clenched and he had a "tight face."

Some of this newfound aggression could have stemmed from Tim being unmoored from his church. Scott Tayler took over the helm of the First Unitarian Church, and Christine didn't like him. She remarked to Tim that she thought the ministers were evil, and she didn't understand how so many parishioners put up with the changes they were making. For two decades the couple had been an integral part of their church choir, and while they sang with Madrigalia after leaving the Unitarian Church, they no longer belonged to that community. At a time when so many things were going wrong in his life, Tim had chosen a path of further isolation.

With all of these changes happening, his Spock-like nature masked the true depth of his problems from Christine. Tim never admitted that he needed help, and she never asked the obvious question: "Tim, what's wrong?" To this day, he does not know why she didn't. Tim pondered, "I don't know what Christine thought or felt. She was often very ginger about asking me how I was coming with the dissertation. I kind of wish she would have just asked, 'What the hell is going on?'"

On top of all of his mounting difficulties, Tim was very worried about his eldest sister, Judy. She and her family had built a house on the family farm in Croton, Ohio. For many years they shared a wonderful family enclave. Marilee converted the barn to her home, and Judy and her family lived next door. Their parents lived in the farmhouse where Tom was raised.

Judy was only in her early sixties, but back in 2001 her doctor had discovered that she had non-Hodgkin lymphoma. She received several years of treatment, including an infusion of her own stem cells, and was in remission for a few years. However, Judy's cancer came back. To make matters worse, the doctors at the Arthur G. James Cancer Hospital at the Ohio State University said that an infusion of her own cells would not be possible a second time.

Chances of finding a compatible stem-cell donor were best among siblings. Tim and James came to Ohio, and the four siblings all went for testing. Tim reminisced, "I remember how great it felt to be together—all there were willing to help. I knew that if any of us were compatible donors, the donation would be from all of us. I remember thinking how strange it was to feel so good about a doctor's appointment to gather lots of blood samples. But it was a great afternoon. I was a match, so I stood ready if the doctors decided another stem-cell transplant was possible."

Tim drove to Ohio in the summer of 2009 for some final tests and to pick up medication to stimulate white blood-cell production. Judy accompanied him during the long day at the hospital. Soon came the news that they were going ahead. Back in New York, Tim started taking the prescribed medications, which required three injections each day for ten days. "Christine was rather quiet about the whole thing," he said. "She watched as I injected myself. A few days into the regimen she offered to do the injections." He allowed her to take over.

Christine had not gone with Tim during the previous visits. She had always been reluctant to go for any longer than a weekend. She came with Tim, however, on the trip to do the infusion. Marilee and Tim drove to the hospital. Tim described the procedure as "not bad—just uncomfortable." He lay in a bed with a tube pulling blood from his left arm into a machine and back through a tube into his right wrist. Tim had to stay hooked up to the machine for six or seven hours. Afterward, the doctors declared that the day of harvesting had produced an adequate amount for one infusion.

"Marilee and I headed back to the farm," Tim went on. "By the time we got there forty-five minutes later, a call had come in saying that the infusion was already performed, and Judy was responding very badly. Marilee and Christine and I drove back to the center [hospital]. Wes, Judy's husband, told us that she was resting and that they had been so frightened, but the doctors said it was not unusual and that now we must wait."

Tim and Christine drove back to Rochester the next day.

He called often to get updates, but none of them was very positive. It looked as though Judy had accepted the stem-cell infusion from Tim's bone marrow, but the amount was not enough to kill the cancer.

"Christine was unusually quiet through the months when it came to Judy's condition," Tim recalled. He believed she was worried about the risk of the procedure, even though Dr. Conners and the doctors at the Ohio hospital had told them there was very little danger for Tim. Christine preferred not going to the farm, but at the same time she didn't like being alone. She wanted to make the trips as short as possible, citing one obligation or another to return to Rochester, such as missing Riley or having to attend a meeting. Despite her lack of moral support, Tim continued to go. "He never wanted to let anyone down," his first wife, Carrie, remarked. "He always gave 120 percent."

The façade of normalcy in Tim and Christine's lives was becoming more brittle each day. They maintained their old habits. Yet Christine found more and more things to complain about. "She was more irritated with things, like the voice of certain commentators on the radio, or the sibilant *s* sound drove her nuts," Tim said. "She would call from the other room, and I would go to the radio and turn it down." She especially hated "the 'zoom-zoom' commercial," a popular Mazda advertisement at the time. Tim remarked, "It drove her nuts."

Christine even complained more and more that the clicking of Tim's computer keys was bothering her. "I didn't understand. 'Why does this bother you so much?'" he recalled asking. "And she would just say it drives her nuts. So I'd let it go."

Curiously, the sound of her own keyboard didn't bother her. It was only Tim's that she found fault with.

Ever submissive, Tim tried to correct the problem, to no avail. "I didn't know what to do about it because I had gone through five different keyboards to try and find one that was quiet," he said. "I couldn't hear the difference between mine and hers. So I got to the point where that wasn't going to help."

Computers were Tim's livelihood. Why would she demand that he not type on his computer? As with all else, though, he chose to overlook her animosity. He was determined to keep up appearances. "She was a person I wanted to be with, and I just knew that I couldn't keep up with the expectations I believed she had of me."

Timothy Wells had not reached bottom yet, though. A succession of events in the terrible fall of 2009 would drive him beyond depression to a state where he was barely connected to any hope that things could get better. He was entering a twilight zone from which he could see only one way out, and that was death.

CHAPTER 7

"THIS HAS TO END"

The last fall in Christine Sevilla's life began with a happy family reunion. For Labor Day weekend, both of her brothers—Chuck from San Diego and Michael from Michigan—came to visit with their wives. The Sevilla clan had a wonderful time together. Chuck remembered that Christine delighted in taking them to her favorite parks. While on the trails, she often stopped to point out tiny flowers or invasive weeds for which none of them, save her, knew the names. In her photographs, she illuminated many of these seemingly insignificant flowers and weeds as beautiful works of nature.

Disconnected as always, Tim receded easily into the background. He did not mar the family reunion with his worries for his own sister, now on her deathbed. All seemed to be normal between him and Christine. During the weekend, "there was never any hint of discord or problems in their marriage," Michael's wife, Donna, later remarked. "They appeared to be mutually supportive."

That façade was ripped away two days later. On September 9, 2009, Judy passed away, at the age of sixty-four. Tim immediately found someone to cover his RIT classes so they could leave town for the wake and funeral. Yet Christine told Tim she wanted to stay for their usual Sunday-night Madrigalia rehearsal. As a result, they missed the wake. After the rehearsal, they drove long into the night in order get to Judy's funeral service. Tim was "disappointed but not angry" with Christine. When asked why he did not attend his sister's wake without Christine, he said he never considered this option.

Because Tim was so guarded with his feelings, his grief was hard to detect. Soon after the funeral, he met with Dr.

Conners for a routine office visit. However, Tim did not
display a lot of reactive symptoms, nor did he appear to be
over-grieving. He didn't ask Dr. Conners for any assistance
during his office visit either.

Yet those who knew Tim well realized what a great loss
Judy's death was to him. "Tim idolized his family," Carrie
remarked. "Losing his sister was huge. It was the most
devastating thing that could have happened to him."

Paula Bataille also noticed what a blow this was to Tim.
She said seeing him so down was terribly sad. "He was a very
defeated person." Still, Paula did not see any outward signs
of significant depression during that fall, although she did
notice that Tim had been drinking more heavily.

Tim's ability to work dropped off from its already anemic
level. He was barely paying attention to the classes he
was teaching, and all work on his Ph.D. ground to a halt.
"Christine would ask how my dissertation was coming," he
said later. "I could always say I was working on it."

That lie would end on November 11, with the undeniable e-mail notification that Fielding Institute had formally
dropped him from their Ph.D. program. The dean of
psychology wrote, "This letter is to inform you that you have
not met Fielding's minimum progress requirements in the
media psychology doctoral program in the School of Psychology. As a result, we will be withdrawing you from the program
effective October 31, 2009." The letter also noted that Tim
had not completed the necessary coursework and confirmed
he'd had difficulties fully contributing to discussions.

Knowing from this e-mail that a certified letter confirming
his dismissal was coming in the regular mail, Tim made
sure he was at home to intercept this letter, to prevent
Christine from learning about his failure. "I didn't want her
to be disappointed in me. I told her I had completed the

coursework." He was terrified that she would be outraged if she found out that he had lied to her.

Tim's fear that Christine would never forgive him had some justification. Others who knew the couple felt that her identity was tied to things like his position at RIT. Paula believed that Christine would never accept his Ph.D. failure. A family member said Christine "demanded a certain image of their marriage" and wanted them to be seen as the perfect couple. Because of this, Tim was unwilling to share with Christine the news of his termination from Fielding or the debt he had accrued.

The amount of Tim's debt was eye opening. For the first two years, his Fielding tuition had largely been covered by RIT. Yet as the years rolled on, so did his debt mount. Tim stopped looking at the Fielding tuition statements, making it easier for him in the short term to extend his student loans without having to face his growing financial jeopardy. But turning a blind eye to this problem was a grave mistake. As of April 20, 2009, Tim's loans totaled $64,330. On top of this, they were now a dead loss, since he would not earn his Ph.D. Tim's annual salary was only $82,000, so paying off the loans was a forbidding prospect.

On top of that, Lumin Guild had been losing money the past two years. On the couple's 2008 tax return, they reported a business loss of $10,821. Tim expected the 2009 loss would be virtually the same. This was another sizable burden for the beleaguered professor, especially when he couldn't even be certain he would keep his job much longer.

Christine herself had expressed concerns about Lumin Guild's finances on several occasions. Tim related how she'd feel down, saying she wasn't bringing any money into the household. He'd tell her they were doing fine. They were in the black, and she was doing such good and creative things.

Tim firmly believed in the credo that a man should shoulder a family's financial obligations. The very thought of Christine having to work just to make money for the household made him feel like a complete failure. Tim put on his happy face, disingenuously telling her, "Look, we're going to be fine. Look, we're putting money away for retirement; the house is pretty much paid off."

As Tim's defeats at work piled up, he devoted more of his waning energy to serving as her Sherpa. "Christine often asked if I had to go into RIT. She would be very disappointed if I had to." Tim spent less and less time on campus. He loved taking care of Christine and being wanted by her.

With storm clouds gathering all around him, Tim finally admitted to himself that he had less energy, less motivation, and less drive, all symptoms of a significant depression. He made a vain attempt to fix his problems by trying to redeem the sample coupon for testosterone that his doctor had given him back in July. Yet by that time, the offer had expired, as had the prescription. Tim was too ashamed to call Dr. Conners and ask for a new prescription.

He remained unaware of the true depths to which his depression was taking him. Only after the murder did mental-health professionals inform Tim he was clinically depressed. They started him on Lexapro, an antidepressant, to lessen the probability of suicide.

All he knew in those waning autumn days was that his burdens just wouldn't stop piling up. After his master's-degree program was canceled, Tim was assigned to teach two new courses for RIT's second trimester, beginning on November 30, 2009: "Themes in Information Technology and Process Management" and "Web Implementation and Human Factors." He gathered material from the professor who previously taught these courses. Looking through it, he noticed that both programs extensively used Adobe Flash, and he'd been struggling to learn that. In a halfhearted effort to prepare for these courses, Tim bought several instructional books, but all the while he kept thinking, "I don't know how I can ever answer questions about any of this." He had simply fallen too far behind.

With the pressure mounting, Tim's insomnia progressed from an occasional nuisance to a nightly specter. He would awaken tense and anxious, drenched in his own sweat. Christine was lying right next to him in bed, yet he could not tell her that he was feeling so troubled and unable to sleep. He kept repeating the same impotent mantra he had told himself so many times before: "Everything is okay. I can handle it." These empty words, however, only added to his turmoil.

Riley became a useful way for him to escape these awful nighttime sessions of lying completely awake. She slept at the foot of the bed with Christine and Tim, and she would often sneak up closer to them. "As the night went on," Tim recalled, "I remember feeling so good that Riley would snuggle up with me."

Conveniently, Riley developed a problem with a weak bladder at night. She would wake up her masters around two or three o'clock, whining to go outside. Predictably, it became Tim's job to let her out. They would go outside and he would look at the stars for a while, hoping to find in them some measure of peace. Yet even after Riley's problem was controlled, Tim used this as an excuse to get out of bed in the early morning hours because he did not want Christine to realize that he was feeling anxious and unable to sleep. He typically was able to get back to sleep within half an hour, and for that reason, he did not take any sleeping pills.

At those times when Tim was able to sleep, he often had vivid and recurring anxiety dreams. "The general pattern was going into a business office thinking I worked there but not being sure if I did. Sometimes I would talk with security officers, where one guard would recognize me but another couldn't find me in their system. Or I'd find my desk, but my coworkers didn't recognize me. Sometimes I'd be talking to someone about a project I was working on, and he'd say that project ended years ago. Often I couldn't find my way around. The odd thing about these dreams was that they spilled over into waking hours. I'd think that maybe there was a company where I had started working at and then just stopped, or I had been hired but never showed up after the initial interview. I had the eerie, uneasy feeling that I had forgotten something so important. It lasted several hours after I woke up."

Tim continued to hide his troubles through the Thanksgiving weekend. That year, the couple and Riley went over to the house of a good friend of Christine's, Ernie's sister, Julia. She was not aware that anything was amiss with Tim and Christine, although she did not have very much contact with either of them, as she was busy hosting the dinner. However, Julia's cousin, Rhonda, had a long conversation with Christine. She recalled that Christine complained about a bad year because Tim had donated bone marrow in a futile effort to save his dying sister. Christine also remarked that she realized she would have to increase her marketing efforts for Lumin Guild, and she hated the thought of that. Rhonda thought Christine was beautiful, opinionated, but negative, yet she was very fond of the couple.

No one noticed that anything had changed between the couple. Even with disaster looming due to Tim's complete failure to prepare for the upcoming trimester, he kept up appearances. "We're told that on Thanksgiving, four days before he strangled her," Donna Sevilla said later, "they held hands on the sofa of family friends."

The long holiday weekend passed, and still Tim made only

halfhearted attempts to prepare for courses he knew he could not teach. The height of his procrastination was reached the night before classes were to begin. Tim made a final attempt to work on them. Writing out each syllabus was easy, because he merely had to update them from the previous section. Yet he still wasn't confident that he could answer any questions the students might raise or even lead the class. Tim was afraid he was going to fail in front of his students. He knew he should read more on the topics, but there was so much he didn't know by this point that the task was overwhelming.

Instead, he decided to accompany Christine to their weekly Sunday-night Madrigalia rehearsal. He excused himself one more time from preparing for class because the rehearsal was important. It was the dress rehearsal for a concert they had coming up the following Sunday, a program featuring Christmas music, to be held at a church in nearby Canandaigua. They had an hour and a half of music to run through. As with Christine's photography jaunts, Tim used a personal occasion to avoid his professional duties.

The Final Night

The guilt of that irresponsibility weighed on him heavily that night after they retired to bed. He kept thinking about the two new classes, the first starting at 10:00 A.M. and the second at 12:30. He slept lightly, waking up at three o'clock and then again at five. By then, he couldn't tolerate lying there another minute. He nudged Riley lightly to wake her up and then let her out the back door, to cover up for the fact that he was the one who really wanted to get up. He stood on the patio for a few minutes, continuing to worry about the classes that morning. Yet he couldn't prepare for them when he'd had so little sleep. He went back to bed and lay there, exhausted, until the alarm went off at six thirty. He got up, made coffee, and fed Riley, trying to pretend today was just like every other day.

It wasn't, though. He couldn't face those students. He brought Christine her coffee and toast in their bedroom at seven, as usual. While eating, they listened to NPR together before getting dressed. Then Christine went out into the living room to check her e-mail, part of her morning routine. At 8:27 A.M., she forwarded one to her friend Steven concerning the latest developments with the county parks commission.

>To: Steven Daniel
>From: Christine <christine.sevilla@gmail.com>
>Just sent this. Hope other attendees of Tuesday's meeting will weigh in. Christine

>From: Christine <christine.sevilla@gmail.com>
>To: Mary Anna Towler at Rochester City News
>Subject: Greece Canal Park Master Plan meeting
>Editor:
>Why is the County's Capital Improvement Program providing $2 million for Greece Canal Park? The next park scheduled for planning activity was widely thought to be Powder Mills Park, so this announcement was unexpected. Our County and Parks Administration owe the public a fair and transparent assessment of resident needs and park resources. Instead, another public "input" meeting was announced just days ahead for a time when the fewest possible can attend: two days before Thanksgiving . . .
>Christine Sevilla
>Perinton

Steven replied, "I think it is a great letter. If they print it it will at least keep the issue out there. Did you see another county presentation on mitigation is scheduled for Saturday?"

When Christine was done, Tim suggested that they go swimming together at their local YMCA. He knew that if he were to prepare for his first class at ten o'clock, he would have to leave for RIT by eight at the latest. Instead, Tim accompanied Christine to the YMCA at eight thirty, leaving just minutes after she got done checking her e-mail. They performed their usual exercise routines. Tim also took a sauna and they swam. Curiously, Christine seemed oblivious to Tim's end-stage procrastination.

While swimming, they encountered their friend Susan, whom they both knew from the YMCA. Susan described Christine as a very passionate person, argumentative and exhausting on issues she believed in. After packing up their things, the threesome left the gym together. Susan walked Tim and Christine to their car. After the murder, when interviewed by the police, she denied noticing any marital tension between the couple that morning.

It was about 10:00 A.M. when Tim and Christine arrived back at Springwood Lane. He told her that he felt really badly about not being ready to teach his new classes. Offering superficial reassurance, Christine placated Tim. "You'll be fine. You always do well." Later, during the police interrogation, Tim contradicted this recollection by saying, "I couldn't go to class and . . . she . . . didn't say anything."

Christine was unaware of the dangerous state of mind her husband had slipped into. And there was scant reason to be aware of it, because Tim had always been the logical one who controlled his emotions.

Tim wandered around the living room, looking out the floor-to-ceiling windows. He noticed Christine sitting at her laptop, and he knew he should at least make an attempt to go through the motions of his usual routine. Rather than hurrying to leave for class, he went about his customary tasks. He threw a load of dirty clothes on the laundry floor, carried the clean ones back to their closet, and straightened up the bed. That was what he always did. "We got home from the Y and we put things away."

Tim left the bedroom and went into the den. He slipped

his computer into his laptop bag as he always did when he had classes. Then he set his bag near the garage door. This is where he usually put his gear before heading out. But Tim knew it was already past the time he was supposed to leave. "I don't understand that," he said in retrospect. "I knew it was past the time, and yet I packed up my computer as if I was going to go, but I knew I wasn't going."

Tim didn't head out the door but instead wandered back into the living room. He had reached a point of no return. He couldn't face going to class and finally exposing himself as a fraud. But he couldn't tell Christine he wasn't going. He grew increasingly desperate. He didn't want to disappoint her. He couldn't let her know what a miserable failure he had become.

Tim concluded with growing certainty that the best thing to do was to kill himself. Then, with the flick of a knife, his miseries, along with his life, would be eliminated. Tim recalled, "I could not get myself to leave the house. Christine was getting ready to leave. I knew I would be dead when she came back."

Christine had a meeting planned with Steven Daniel to discuss the county parks commission. Just minutes before her death, she sent what would be her last e-mail, which lacked any hint of the horror that was about to transpire.

To: Steven Daniel
From: Christine <christine.sevilla@gmail.com>
Subject: Re: Greece Canal Park Master Plan meeting
Date: November 30, 2009 9:55:47 AM
They have an excuse not to print it, I realize. But if someone else who attended would write it might give the Rochester City Newspaper a push. Still unlikely the editor will be interested in ruffling feathers, although a letter conveys a viewpoint she doesn't have to espouse. I wonder if anyone is attending that Dec 5 research conference, and who it is

presenting about the County mitigation wetland plan. I asked Peter if he was attending. I hope so. I can't attend (too late to register anyway)—maybe something will be posted about the sessions.

As Tim recalled, Christine headed into the galley kitchen after she sent the e-mail. Tim, standing helplessly by the windows facing the backyard, saw her pick up the portable phone on the counter. He guessed she was going to call Steven, since she usually called the person she was meeting before she went out. She was getting ready to leave for the local Starbucks, because that's where she often met people.

The sight of her leaving filled Tim with panic. He wasn't going to class, but how could he let her go, knowing that he was about to end his own life? Or worse, what if she left and never came back? He couldn't tolerate the thought of her being disappointed. Out of nowhere he felt a wall looming before him. He remembered how often Christine had said to him, "Thank God you are here." He did everything around the house. He bought the groceries, cooked the meals, and prepared Riley's special duck dinners. He desperately wanted to believe that Christine could not manage without him, that she would never leave him. For her sake, it was better if she came with him, where he was going. "This has to end," he thought.

He walked toward her, filled with a new resolve, and she headed into the mudroom at the far end of the kitchen. The small room, with a washer and dryer placed in an adjoining walk-in closet, had a fold-down ironing board mounted on the laundry-room door. On the diamond-tiled floor lay the pile of dirty clothes, heaped on top of a rumpled sheet. According to Tim's recollection, Christine pulled a light coat out of the closet and shrugged into it. She had the phone in her hand, punching in the numbers to make a call. He came right up to her—and clamped both his hands around her neck.

She looked astonished. "What are you doing?!" she stammered.

He moved his hands higher and held on tight, so hard that Christine gasped. As he pressed harder with his long, skinny fingers, she was startled, dumbfounded, then bewildered by what now possessed her meek husband, but she didn't resist. Tim recalled that Christine merely hit his arms gently for him to stop. With his grip like iron, he slowly lowered his much smaller wife to the floor, so that she was lying on her back. She clutched his arms, but gradually her arms dropped away.

Tim had no idea how long he squeezed his hands around her delicate neck. "I was over her and held her throat for some time. Her eyes glaze over. Her tongue swells. I don't know how long I hold her. Five minutes? Fifteen minutes? I just hold her throat. I have never been able to put a duration to this. It felt loving." At last, Tim let his hands relax. Beyond all doubt, Christine was dead. As Tim stood up, he noticed the phone on the floor. He picked it up and replaced it in the kitchen cradle.

As a child, Timothy Wells had tried so hard to be a good boy. In his first marriage, he tried so hard to be a model husband. After his disgraceful failures at the end of their marriage, Tim was determined that, the second time around, he would finally get it right. He submitted to his second wife in order to maintain the appearance of a blissful marriage. The only flaw in his plan was his failed self. The mounting losses and terrible secrets that threatened this perfect image gradually overwhelmed him. He would tell homicide detectives that despite all his efforts, "nothing was working." In the suicide note he penned after Christine's murder, he reached the logical, terrible conclusion: "I killed the one I loved because I was a failure."

CHAPTER 8

WHEN THE SONG WAS OVER

Timothy Wells' daylong odyssey to determine the right spot for the pack to end arrived at its ignominious conclusion early the next morning. As snow began to fall on Mendon Ponds park, the drunken professor was placed in the back of a police car. He was taken to the Monroe County Public Safety Building and ushered into a fourth-floor interview room at 3:36 A.M. He was given a glass of water and then left to wait. Tim spent the next eleven hours in that sterile room. That gave him plenty of time to consider the enormity of what he had done.

Investigator Scott Walsh was ready to interview him at 5:09 that morning. The tiny room that held Professor Wells was wired for video and audio recordings. Investigator Walsh read Tim his Miranda rights, and then asked, "Do you understand each of these rights that I have explained to you?" Tim said that he did. Walsh then asked, "Having these rights in mind, do you wish to talk to me now?"

"Yeah, I'm willing to talk now," Tim responded.

The goal of interviewing a person suspected of a crime is to obtain a confession, and Tim was all too ready to comply. Investigator Walsh proceeded to ask Tim what had happened during the terrible day before, and Tim told him everything. As with the police officers earlier that day, Tim frequently broke down. Oddly, several times during the interrogation, he referred to Christine in the present tense, even though he had just confessed to murdering her, and would vacillate back to talking about her in the past tense.

Investigator Walsh's summation would read:

He stated in sum and substance that on November 30, 2009 at about 1000 hours he strangled his wife Christine. He further stated that they did not have an argument. Wells also stated that he placed his deceased wife in the trunk of his car and drove around for several hours. He then stated that he drove her to the area of Devil's Bathtub in Mendon Ponds Park. He planned to place her there, kill their dog Riley, and then kill himself. He hit the dog on the head with a rock and felt he killed her, and then realized that he did not know how to end his own life. It was at that point that he called 911.

Among the key points of Investigator Walsh's interview was when Tim blurted out the words necessary to lock down the case: "I strangled my wife." Walsh also tried in vain to uncover his motive for the murder. Puzzled, Tim stammered, "I couldn't go to class. . . . I don't know why. I don't know why." The same bizarre reasoning that had overtaken him the morning before emerged again in his talk with the investigator. "We were all supposed to just die." Asked why, Tim replied, "Nothing was working."

The investigator pressed Tim. "You said that you thought about this for a couple of years?" Tim replied in fragmented statements that he had been thinking of a way out for a couple of years. Only the unique circumstances of that Monday had finally shaped this passing notion into the frightening reality.

By 5:40, a mere half-hour after Investigator Walsh entered interview room number two, he had what he needed to refer the case to the district attorney. He was very satisfied with his work. At that point, the detective left the room, and although he stopped back in several times during that long morning to clarify a few points, Tim had already sealed his fate.

The police were taking no chances, however. A few minutes before 11:00 A.M., a second detective entered the interview room. "Hi, you haven't met me yet," he said, introducing himself to Tim. "I'm Greg Woodworth. I'm an investigator with the sheriff's office. I do the computer forensics." He then asked Tim which computers he and Christine used, what their passwords were, and the login information for the Lumin Guild Web site. He wanted to read the couple's e-mails, social-media pages, and all Web sites they visited for any evidence possibly related to the murder. Tim promptly provided all the answers he needed, and Mr. Woodworth exited seventeen minutes later.

In the meantime, Investigator Steve Peglow, another member of the Major Crimes Unit, fielded a call at approximately 11:00. A man named Don Bataille wished to speak to a detective. When Investigator Peglow called him, Don volunteered that he was a neighbor of the couple, and he thought he had a voicemail message from Christine on the morning of the murder. At 11:45, Investigator Peglow arrived at Don Bataille's place of employment in downtown Rochester, an architectural firm, and he recorded the voice message on a handheld digital recorder. According to the phone's caller ID information, this call was received sometime after 9:24 A.M., just shortly before the murder.

It later turned out that Don Bataille was mistaken— Christine hadn't called him. Yet Peglow had to follow up on any potential leads, and at 12:50, he appeared in Tim's interview room and played the recording for Tim to hear. Tim mistakenly believed that the voice on the recording was Christine's, further volunteering that she'd had their home telephone in her hand when he grabbed her. To this day, if Christine had actually called someone moments before her death, the identity of the caller remains unknown.

Shortly before then, at 12:30, Investigator Walsh arrived at 4 Springwood Lane in Pittsford to execute a search warrant on their house. The warrant had been signed by Judge John Connell, and police officers had secured the premises. After searching the scene of the crime, Walsh went to RIT at 2:45 to search Tim's office. This was brief, and he exited at 3:22.

By this time, the detectives were very confident they had a strong case. At 2:35, Investigator Peglow handcuffed Tim behind his back, and they exited the interview room. He and another detective transported Wells to the Perinton Town Court for his arraignment. The *Democrat and Chronicle* reported, "Escorted into the courtroom by several sheriffs deputies, clad in an oversized tan jail jumpsuit and orange jacket, Wells looked frazzled with bewildered eyes and messy gray hair." He was charged with second-degree murder. During the brief session before Justice Thomas A. Klonick, Tim told the judge he neither had a lawyer nor knew of one. A plea of not guilty was entered, and the judge ordered Tim held behind bars until he could find an attorney and petition for bail.

With a single act that defied logic, Tim Wells murdered his wife and became a ward of the state. (From *Democrat and Chronicle,* December 11, 2009, © 2009 Gannett, www.democratandchronicle.com. All rights reserved. Used by permission and protected by the Copyright Laws of the United States. The printing, copying, redistribution, or retransmission of this Content without express written permission is prohibited.)

The victim in this sad case had meanwhile been brought to the morgue. After Tim had been taken away early that morning, a tow truck arrived on the scene to retrieve the Saturn stuck in its muddy spot on the hill. Once the vehicle was winched onto the lower parking lot, the medical examiner, Dr. Caroline Dignan, removed Christine's body from the trunk. Her body was blue and purple from lying all day and night in the cold. It was placed on a gurney and taken away for an autopsy that would last nearly five hours.

Dr. Dignan's external examination focused on the head and neck area, as could be expected in a case of manual strangulation. What was evident right away was a series of petechial hemorrhages on Christine's face and in her eyes. These are tiny, pinpoint, red marks that indicate asphyxia caused by an external means of obstructing a person's airways. These marks can be found in murders involving strangulation, hanging, and smothering. Another indicator that strangulation was the likely cause of death was intramuscular bleeding in her tongue. The medical examiner also found numerous bruises of the muscles and soft tissues in Christine's neck.

All of this evidence could not be reconciled with Tim's version of his gentle, loving murder. Dr. Dignan found physical evidence that completely contradicted his story. Most prominent was a one-by-four-inch scalp and subgaleal hemorrhage on the back of her head. Such a wound could not have been caused simply by Christine's head striking the floor. The symmetry of the wound strongly suggested that Tim forcefully struck her with a blunt object before strangling her. Then, while she was either disoriented or unconscious, he strangled her. Another fact that supports this version is the total lack of defense wounds on Tim's body. Anyone being strangled will struggle violently for their life. Yet Tim escaped with nary a scratch.

No one could believe it. Everyone who knew the couple was stunned. Allen Hopkins, a local folksinger in

Heartland Concerts, told the *Democrat and Chronicle*, "It seems unfathomable. When something like this happens that is so unexpected and out of character, it makes you start looking around and saying . . . who else do we know that could do something like this out of the clear blue sky?"

People knew Tim as a gentle, caring husband. Paul Malatesta, Christine's first husband, had stayed in touch with her through the years, and he told the newspaper, "I remember her writing to the effect that she had the sweetest, most caring husband imaginable. I've tried to construct some plausible explanation why a person described as the most considerate husband imaginable could do something like this."

No one had any reason to believe they were unhappy with each other, and no one came forth with any stories that either of them was cheating on the other. Photographer Dan Neuberger told the paper that Tim's actions were "totally incongruous" with the "nice, intelligent, helpful man" he knew. Tim was the last person Don expected to be violent.

Patricia Knoll and other neighbors on Springwood Lane were shocked when they saw the crime-scene tape strung around the house. "They were fine neighbors, nice people . . . it really comes as a shock," she told local reporters. Tanya Pattison, another neighbor, told the paper she'd just seen Christine a few days before and she had been smiling as usual. "She came over on Thanksgiving and brought us some artwork she had been working on."

Their friends in the environmental movement were floored. "It's a surprise to me, because she and Tim Wells . . . seemed like such gentle people," Jim Howe, executive director of the local Nature Conservancy chapter, told the paper. "This couple was the most genteel couple I have ever met," agreed June Summers, president of Genesee Valley Audubon Society. "This is so uncharacteristic."

The Reverend Richard Gilbert, Tim's former pastor,

agreed. He told the newspaper that Tim and Christine made beautiful music together. "It's totally out of character," he said of the murder charge. "We're all devastated because we loved them both. They were a beautiful couple." On further reflection, he added, "Everything we believed about couples being able to fall in love at first sight, we want to believe that's possible. Tim and Christine were the sort of couple that made us believe in that, and we don't want to let this go."

Astonishment was matched by the deep sorrow felt by Christine's family. Michael Sevilla related how he learned the news that no brother should ever have to receive. "On December 1, 2009, two police officers came to our home to inform me that my sister had been murdered by her husband. Disbelief, then a crushing feeling of horror, filled me. I called my brother and we called my father to break the news. These phone calls were painful beyond words."

His wife, Donna, couldn't believe something so horrible could happen. "Tim Wells was welcomed into our family and spent much time with us in family vacations in northern California, Manhattan, Mexico, and Spain," she later wrote. "Over the years, our family heard all sorts of laudatory comments about how 'Tim did this' and 'Tim was able to do that' or 'Tim thinks thus and such.' Christine was loyal and never complained about Tim. They seemed so perfectly matched." She thought they had an excellent relationship. Christine was so happy and so was Tim, or so Donna and Michael believed. "Even with the benefit of hindsight we're not able to look back and reinterpret things." Donna later turned bitter. Although Tim's family members reached out to the Sevilla family, to this day they have never received an apology or explanation from Tim.

Devastation and grief spread throughout the Sevilla family and among all those who had known Christine. Meanwhile, the fate of the couple's poor dog, Riley, was still undetermined. Tim had not killed Riley, although he had inflicted several horrifying wounds on the top of her head. Before he had been taken from the Devil's Bathtub to police headquarters, he told officers that Riley's body could be found by the park bench overlooking the pond. Yet in the darkness and swirling snow, the police investigators couldn't find her. At 7:31 that morning, Investigator Walsh reentered the interview room where Tim was being held to ask him exactly where the bench was. With the information he provided, the dog was finally found on a nearby trail. According to Deputy Diaz's report, a crime-scene technician observed that Riley had blood on her snout and the top of her head. Near where Riley was found, the weapon, a large rock covered with fresh blood, was photographed and collected for evidence. To Tim's great relief and surprise, Walsh returned to the interview room at 7:41 and reported Riley had been found and was still alive. As Tim recalled his brutal attack on Riley, he was certain she was dead.

The police called Joel Taylor, the head of Mendon Town Hall Dog Control, and he soon arrived at the Devil's Bathtub. Riley was placed in the backseat of a police car and taken directly to the Suburban Animal Hospital. The staff there immediately began to clean and stitch up her head wounds.

Over the next several days, Christine's longtime friend, Ernie Lederman, called about Riley. At first he offered to take the dog, but then Nora Bredes and her son stepped in. They were aware of Riley's food allergies and promised to provide a good home. They already had a dog, but her son Gabriel, then fourteen, insisted they take Riley. She was finally convinced when he said, "Mom, if we get to adopt Riley, it will be the most important thing our family has ever done." Three days after the murder, they picked up Riley from the animal hospital.

Nora did not want her son to see how badly the dog was injured, but nothing could disguise the deep, raw gashes on Riley's head. She'd suffered hemorrhages in her mouth, ears, and eyes. Nora later wrote to Judge Joan Kohout that at the time, they couldn't be sure Riley would recover from the trauma. Riley seemed not to have lasting neurological damage, but only time would tell. Nora recalled, "Gabe and I talked for hours over the next days about how anyone could so brutally injure this sweet, playful dog. While I may have identified with Christine, Gabe identified with Riley. As he put it, 'Riley was like their only child. How could a dad do this?'"

Soon after hearing the horrific news of her murder, the First Unitarian Church held an evening vigil for Christine. Despite the couple having left the church a few years earlier, hundreds of people attended to express their grief. Tim and Christine had, after all, been members of the congregation for more than two decades. Everyone sat quietly for an hour, lost in their reflections on what Christine had meant to each of them. They exchanged hugs and kisses all around, with tears running down their cheeks. They lit candles and wrote remembrances of her in books provided by the church, so that she would never be forgotten. The Reverend Scott Tayler told the local paper, "I think I speak for all of us here that the enormity, the depth of this loss and this tragedy, has taken us all beyond words, and beyond the ability to make sense of it all."

For Tim, the following day would prove to be a busy one. So far he had been held in solitary confinement under a suicide watch. Tim underwent a psychiatric evaluation by Dr. Robert Stern and was found to have "major depressive disorder with narcissistic traits." Dr. Stern also determined that Tim had projected his fear of failure onto Christine. Dr. Stern felt that, under the circumstances, Tim might be able to plead temporary insanity during his trial. Later, Tim met with and retained James Nobles, the defense lawyer he selected to represent him in court. Tim planned to pay for Mr. Nobles' services by tapping into his retirement nest egg. These were the same dollars that had been set aside for Tim and Christine's golden years. The

district attorney's office subsequently brought the case before
a Monroe County grand jury, and Tim was indicted for felony
murder in the second degree.

Throughout his first weeks in jail, Tim would have a number
of visitors who encouraged him to stay strong. It was clear he
was openly grieving for Christine as well. His most frequent
visitor was his older sister Marilee, who commuted from the
family farm in Ohio. Nobles was very impressed by the number
of people who thought highly enough of Tim to visit him. The
disparity between Tim's many supporters and the gravity of his
crime suggested to Nobles that a plea of temporary insanity was
a possible defense. Clearly, Tim was not a homicidal maniac,
but this did not change the fact that he murdered his wife.

On December 16, 2009, a Wednesday evening, Christine's
family and friends gathered for a memorial service held at
the University of Rochester Interfaith Chapel. The same grief
that had marked her vigil was overwhelming among those who
gathered. In one of the most moving speeches at the memorial,
her brother Chuck said, "Christine defined herself in her
'Watershed' book as a dog lover, singer, photographer, book
artist, information and instructional designer, adjunct professor
at RIT, and author. To that list may be added ardent defender
of the wetlands, the trails, and parks. In that defense, she was
a light, revealing to those who would look, the land's hidden
beauty and the need for its preservation. I think Christine's last
message to us tonight would be this: daily treasure the living,
your loved ones and friends, and this good earth."

Her brother Michael added these words in his speech: "No
one could bear a loss as great as this alone, and it is also so
that Christine's creative and fulfilled life could not have been
lived alone. My sister, Christine, moved to Rochester when
she was a young woman and over the years grew to be a vital
part of this community. . . . For the family, I want to express
our great appreciation and heartfelt thanks to those of you

in the community who have given so much to her. Her loss has been a devastating event in the lives of the family, as so much that was beautiful seems to be lost. One comfort we have found is the outpouring of sympathy and support that we have received from you."

Many others wrote letters for the occasion. Stephen Lewandowski, author and environmentalist, wrote about what Christine's artistic passions represented: "Christine was an artist. The eighteenth century poet and lexicographer Samuel Johnson remarked on the artist's dual role: to instruct and to delight. Christine's special art was to educate us with beautiful images."

Fellow photographer Bruno Chalifour wrote, in part: "She was a very dedicated and hard working person. She applied all her energy, focus, and sensitivity to the areas on which she had set her mind and her heart. In the recent years she had accomplished more in photography and for the environment than most have in a lifetime."

Fellow churchgoer Susan Ames wrote a letter as well, and she recalled how generous Christine was in helping others. "A few years ago I saw an interesting item in our First Unitarian Church newsletter that asked church members to consider joining the 'most fun' committee in the church. As chairperson of the Williams Gallery Art Exhibit Committee, it was Christine's way of trying to entice people to join the committee. Not being an artist myself, yet having an interest in learning more about art, I joined the committee. It has been a wonderful (and fun!) experience for me, and I thank Christine for it."

On December 20, Madrigalia held their annual Christmas concert. It became a way for the choir members to express their grief for Christine. Sadly, she had been scheduled to sing a solo, "Summer in Winter," that reflected on the changing light of the seasons. For her, that light had been forever dimmed.

Three days later, Tim was brought to Monroe County Court

for a hearing. Because the case had gained so much notoriety, his appearance was scheduled early in the day. Before Judge Patricia D. Marks, James Nobles entered a plea of not guilty to a single felony charge of second-degree murder. Tim, dressed in a prison-issued beige jumpsuit, mouthed "thank you" to a handful of friends sitting in the second row of the gallery. Judge Marks ordered that Tim be held without bail, and his next court appearance was scheduled for January 8.

On December 30, Christine's friends in the environmental movement announced that they had started a fund in order to purchase a parcel of undeveloped land and name it after her. "A wetland area in good shape would be ideal," naturalist Steven Daniel told the *Rochester City Newspaper*. The Genesee Land Trust and the Genesee Valley Audubon Society created a fund where donations could be sent in Christine's memory. In addition, the Audubon Society offered to reprint her "Garden Villains" brochure and sell it to raise money for Christine's wetland.

The Mental Evaluations

Several weeks earlier, James Nobles had placed a call to Dr. Jerid Fisher, a forensic neuropsychologist specializing in mental evaluations of individuals accused of felony crimes. Mr. Nobles asked Dr. Fisher if he had seen the case in the news, and Dr. Fisher said he had heard enough bits and pieces from the media to have a biased slant on the case. Tim must be a crazy professor. Mr. Nobles asked Dr. Fisher if, despite being tainted by media reports, he would be able to conduct a fair and unbiased psychological and neuropsychological evaluation of his client. Dr. Fisher knew this meant he had to wipe his mind clean of all preconceptions.

As an expert, when becoming involved in a case, he knew he must put aside any information he had heard as a layperson while making every effort to reject bias. Dr. Fisher found the

Sherlock Holmes nature of forensic psychology to be especially challenging and rewarding. As he began putting together the facts of the case and Tim's version of what happened that day, critical doubts began to arise about Tim's story. Was Tim a liar? Or was he lying to himself? The doctor would get his first opportunity to address these questions in a meeting with Tim scheduled for January 14.

Before their first meeting occurred, Tim appeared in court for his next bail hearing, and bail was again refused. First Assistant District Attorney Sandra Doorley said after the second hearing that she was opposed to any further bail requests for Tim. James Nobles said only that he reserved the right to ask for bail at a later date. He still had not discussed a plea bargain with prosecutors yet. He said he received discovery materials just two days before and told the *Democrat and Chronicle*, "We probably won't have an idea where this is going until after the hearing." Asked how Tim was coping with being in jail, Nobles replied, "He's doing very well. He's a very intelligent man. He spends a lot of time reading— materials relevant to his defense, and other materials."

Tim's first session with Dr. Fisher came a week later. An initial interview was followed by a standardized personality test called the Million Clinical Multiaxial Inventory-III. While the testing was routine, Dr. Fisher felt that the professor was anything but ordinary. Dr. Fisher remembered Tim in his orange prison jumpsuit, so different from the typical prisoner he was accustomed to seeing in jail. He looked like a tired, sad professor type, tall, lanky, and bewildered. Tim was very cooperative with Dr. Fisher, eager to talk, and in the first interview Tim told him about many of the losses he had sustained in the prior year. He was frequently tearful and in obvious pain. They stayed away from the murder. This was Dr. Fisher's usual approach when conducting forensic evaluations. He felt there was plenty of time to explore those

issues and believed it was far more important to build rapport
and trust with Tim than to immediately start asking intrusive
and disturbing questions about the homicide.

Dr. Fisher set up a second appointment with Tim to
continue interviewing and testing. Dr. Fisher recalled that
during his second visit with Tim that he had the same sad
and bewildered appearance as their first meeting but was
again eager to talk. Rapport was easily established. Dr. Fisher
remembered some of his early thoughts about Tim being a
well-educated college professor and just a year older than
him. It is easy to understand how these similarities might
color his thinking about Tim. But in assessing an individual it
is critical to avoid these tendencies. However, this was a very
different kind of crime and Tim was a very different criminal.
Tim completed the 567-question Minnesota Multiphasic
Personality Inventory-2 on this visit. By the next day, the
analysis of Tim's personality-test results had been completed.

Among Dr. Fisher's observations, and what stood out in these
early meetings with Tim, was the bizarre dissociation between
that fatal morning and Tim's intellectual distance from his
brutality. Fisher told the *Democrat and Chronicle,* "I think his
anger is so buried that he can't get in touch with it. This is a man
who has spent his whole life running away from anger. Anger
is an emotion that's foreign to him. Anger and violence are so
unacceptable to Tim that he is incapable of acknowledging he
has ever had these feelings." Two years after the murder, Tim
himself was able to reflect, "There are many aspects of my life
and behavior leading to the tragedy I do not understand. The
most troublesome to me is explaining my lack of anger."

Dr. Fisher put on his Sherlock Holmes hat, analyzing the
evidence and blending it with his understanding of Tim's
psychological makeup. Something was off. In the autopsy
photos, Christine was still wearing her gym clothes—gray
sweatpants, black socks, and black Reebok sneakers. That was

odd, because Christine usually dressed very stylishly when she went out. Afterward, Tim described his act of murder as a mercy killing. The medical examiner's autopsy, however, contradicted this incredible claim. It revealed blunt-force injury to the back of Christine's head.

It became clear that Tim's description of Christine's murder, while inaccurate, was not an intentional lie to cover up his actions but represented the desperate attempt of his psyche to actively deny and block out all evidence that her murder was a stark testament to his latent violent capabilities.

Dr. Fisher continued contacts with Tim into late January and early February, during which he ruled out any reasonable possibility of brain damage by administering specific neuropsychological test procedures. He did not expect to find any evidence of brain damage, but it was important for him to rule this out as an expert advising Nobles about a possible defense. Had Dr. Fisher found evidence of brain damage, this discovery could have offered a potential defense or, at the very least, an explanation for this bizarre murder. In an effort to gather more background information on Tim, he conducted phone interviews with the people closest to Tim, including his ex–wife, family members, neighbors, and colleagues.

James Nobles told local reporters that he would challenge the admissibility of Tim's original confession. He said to the *Democrat and Chronicle,* "The main piece of evidence they have is the statement, and we're trying to figure out the context of it and whether it was legally obtained." He cited extenuating circumstances to bolster his challenge to suppress Tim's confession. In particular, he pointed to Tim's disturbed state of mind when he spoke to the detectives.

In court papers, Tim's lawyer argued that Wells was in a psychologically fragile state and did not understand how his confession would be used against him. When reporters queried him about a possible legal defense known as

Extreme Emotional Disturbance, Nobles said, "We're certainly exploring all of our options." In this type of defense, the fact that Tim killed his wife would be conceded. Nobles would try to provide enough evidence, however, that Wells was suffering from so much emotional trauma that there was a reasonable explanation or excuse for his homicidal behavior.

If the jury accepted this argument, the second-degree murder charge would be reduced to first-degree manslaughter, resulting in a significant reduction in the number of years Tim might have to serve time. In New York, second-degree murder carries a mandatory prison term ranging from fifteen years to life, whereas first-degree manslaughter carries a mandatory prison term ranging from five to twenty-five years.

First Assistant District Attorney Sandra Doorley wasn't buying it. She told the local newspaper that all the legal requirements were met in obtaining Tim's confession, so it could be used as evidence against him. She was skeptical of his claim that "the pack had to end"—that he would follow Christine's death by killing himself. She believed he knowingly killed his wife in a fit of rage, then for hours tried to figure out how to hide her body. As for the suicide note found in the car, she remarked to reporters that "nothing in the evidence suggested that he attempted to take his life in any way, shape or form." The prosecution was quick to point out that, after all of the searches, the mysterious knife was never found.

The wheels of justice grind slowly, and Tim continued to languish in jail through the spring and summer and on into the fall. He became a model citizen in prison. Because he was so much better educated than his fellow inmates, Tim began helping several to pursue their high school equivalency diplomas, happy that the inmates needed him.

After the judge declined to suppress Wells' confession, Mr. Nobles asked Dr. Fisher to reenter the case early in the fall, so Dr. Fisher again reviewed all of the available information.

He reviewed the crime-scene details and photographs, the recording of Tim's 911 call, the video of his lengthy police interrogation, the autopsy photographs, his initial interview notes, and his test results. Trying to solve the riddle of the whydunit, Dr. Fisher then interviewed Paula Bataille several times, as well as Dan Neuberger and Dr. Conners. He made multiple visits to the crime scenes at 4 Springwood Lane and the Devil's Bathtub at Mendon Ponds park.

He searched for clues, trying to imagine Christine's final moments on November 30 and taking note of the couple's personal effects that were still in their usual places, as if the house was frozen in time, waiting for them to return. On several occasions, Dr. Fisher drove directly from the Springwood Lane residence to the city jail. It was impossible to ignore the stark contrast between these divergent worlds—the couple's warm suburban home and Tim's cold, sterile prison. This eerie reality was a chilling reminder of everything that was lost that day.

James Nobles accompanied Dr. Fisher one late September day in what would be his final visit with Tim before the upcoming trial. Dr. Fisher asked Tim to consider discrepancies between his description of Christine's murder and the autopsy evidence. He told Tim that his story about how he strangled Christine did not make sense. Rather, the autopsy data strongly indicated that Tim first struck Christine on the back of her head before he strangled her. Tim listened intently and responded that he had no reason to doubt Dr. Fisher's truthfulness, but he still could not accept this version of the facts. Tim prefaced his thoughts by saying, "It went something like this." He asked Fisher and Nobles to imagine a scenario in which Tim had awoken one morning, had eggs for breakfast, and then placed his dirty dish in the sink. Later in this hypothetical, Fisher and Nobles discovered remnants of pancakes, rather than eggs, in the sink. Yet when they asked Tim if he enjoyed his pancakes, he, notwithstanding the tangible evidence, insisted, "I had eggs." Similarly, Tim's memory of Christine's murder was the only version that he could accept.

Dr. Fisher believed that Tim created a version of Christine's death that, in his mind, converted his violent actions toward her into a mercy killing, an act of love. Tim's psychological defenses forced him to twist the facts of Christine's murder into an acceptable narrative for his psyche. The gentleman's gentleman, the Sherpa, the man who likened himself to Spock, had always let others walk all over him with spikes rather than have a confrontation or get angry. He could not accept any evidence that would force him to admit that he was capable not only of anger but also murder. Tim's mind retreated from this reality to maintain the status quo at any cost. He blocked out any memories hinting of rage and substituted a loving and almost blissful narrative. That way, he could deny the brutality of his actions and believe that Christine's murder was a mercy killing. On September 29, almost ten months after the murder, Dr. Fisher completed a detailed psychological report describing his findings for the court.

The Plea

Tim decided that rather than going forward with the trial, he would plead guilty to the second-degree murder charge, sparing both families from a prolonged and painful ordeal. On October 12, 2010, Nobles announced that Tim had pleaded guilty to murder in the second degree. During the formal sentencing hearing that took place on November 19, 2010, almost a year after the murder, Judge Kohout ordered him to serve not less than sixteen years behind bars in a New York state penitentiary.

James Nobles told reporters during the news conference that day that the decision to waive a trial had come only after months of consideration. "There were significant mental-health issues going on at the time for Mr. Wells. However, for his privacy's sake, I'm not going to disclose those details at this time. Our decision to take this plea was a practical one as well as a legal one, because again, even if our extreme emotional defense was found to be valid, he still could have been sentenced to up to twenty-five years in prison, which is certainly more than what he is going to receive under this agreement."

Nobles went on to provide a telling insight into Tim's motives on that bleak morning the previous November. "This is a very unusual case, and the truth of the matter is that Mr. Wells loved his wife, and he continues to love his wife. He continues to grieve his wife on a daily basis. Ultimately, like many people who are considering suicide, at the time they are thinking about those actions, their perception of reality isn't accurate."

First Assistant District Attorney Sandra Doorley was not so forgiving. She called Tim a coward and a monster. In her role as an advocate for the prosecution, she referenced a vague comment Tim made during his interrogation that could have insinuated he had been thinking about killing Christine for quite some time. "To everyone, her marriage to the defendant seemed wonderful and they appeared to be the perfect couple," she said. "But that was certainly not the case. The defendant killed his wife in a narcissistic, prideful, and purposeful act because he was a failure."

Judge Kohout touched on Wells' refusal to ask for help for his mental-health issues as she imposed sentence. "It's hard, I think, for anyone to understand how a well-educated, respected, loving man with no history of violence in his past could do such a thing," she said. "But I would say that in our country, where self-reliance is stressed, asking for help is difficult."

Tim's final, scornful judgment about himself was, "It's clearly just very selfish and prideful of me to think that she couldn't live without me. That's ridiculous." Of course this was crazy. Christine and Riley would do fine without him. Christine may or may not have forgiven him for hiding his student-loan debt and his distress over his career, but that was her right either way. If Tim had quit RIT, Christine may or may not have supported him. But that would be her decision. Tim later acknowledged, "It was not my right to project my assumptions upon her. It was so unfair of me not to be honest and open with Christine. It was me who couldn't bear my failures, not her."

But to this day, Tim's psychological defenses still prevent him from recalling the murder as it actually occurred. "Trying to picture myself as an investigator, I see that things don't make sense. I have no memory of hitting her in any way. I have no memory of struggling or twisting around." No matter how hard Tim tries to put the pieces together, he just can't.

While no one can ever really know with complete certainty what happened that day, it is clear that the hard facts and common sense shape a story very different from Tim's narrative. If there was anything Tim viscerally feared more than his own anger, it was Christine's. The same psychological defenses that allowed him to deny his aggression in murdering Christine also allowed him to block out any hint of her anger or disapproval over the many years of their marriage.

A possible scenario follows. After Christine replied to her friend Steven Daniel at 9:55 A.M., she discovered that Tim hadn't left for RIT to teach his new classes, and a heated disagreement—perhaps a full-blown argument—ensued. Christine, with a flaring temper, insisted that he go to RIT to teach his classes or she would leave. In Tim's disturbed state of mind, the thought of Christine leaving him was the last straw. Tim was out of options. Overwhelmed, he could no longer cope and had hit rock bottom. Then Christine began to leave, still dressed in her gym clothes but too caught up in the moment to stop and change. To prevent her from walking out on him, Tim panicked and impulsively slammed her on the back of her head with the cordless home phone. Once she was incapacitated, he strangled her to death.

Before the sentence was announced, Judge Kohout had asked the family and friends of Christine Sevilla to write letters about the impact her murder had on them. Dozens of letters were submitted. The most touching were those provided by those who loved her most.

Christine's brother Michael wrote:

> Her murder and its aftermath have been traumatic to my family and me in a profound way. I felt horrible that I could not protect her from this horrendous act. My physical state deteriorated. Even though at the memorial I was constantly warned to take care of myself, my blood pressure shot up and I was eventually hospitalized at the beginning of March with multiple blood clots in my leg, which became life threatening. I am now on blood thinners. In March I also became executor of Christine's estate and have had the multiple responsibilities which will extend for several years. A most painful task has been going through Christine's belongings that she had day to day need of and no longer does.

Brother Chuck wrote:

> We hurt because we cannot speak with her, share her e-mails and photos, go on vacations together to enjoy her company, listen to her lovely voice as she would sing to us, and do all the other things that loving brothers and sisters do. She was the glue that held the family together.
>
> With help from her friends, she developed as an accomplished singer and musician. She performed songs in Spanish, Portuguese; she loved jazz, the blues, and songs of humor. She sang with the Unitarian Church Choir and Madrigalia, . . . and we fondly remember vacations and family gatherings where she would sing for us. She did not suffer stage fright. She was fearless.
>
> She was the one who, after a family vacation to Spain, maintained connections with our relatives there. She even

made a return trip by herself to Spain and from that trip came her book, *Memorias,* a meditation on her Spanish roots.

Chuck went on to describe the devastating effect his sister's death had on their father:

> Through this murder, my 92-year-old father lost his only daughter. Telling him of her death was one of the hardest things my brother and I ever had to do. No one should have to give a father such terrible news. He tells me he thinks of Christine every day and I see, hear and feel the pain he bears.
>
> This past year, I have made it a point to talk to him regularly to keep his spirits up. Last weekend, I went to his home in Santa Rosa and asked him to write a letter to you. He made two attempts but was too upset by the process to get more than a paragraph down. So I took over the writing for him and his letter is included with mine. The handwriting is mine; the sentiments are his.

> Dear Judge Kohout,
> I started to write you a letter, but I'm too old and nervous, so my son Chuck is doing this for me.
> I am Christine Diane Sevilla's father. No parent should have to write such a letter because no parent expects to lose their child. Christine was my youngest and my only daughter.
> Christine was precious to me. She was a talented singer, photographer, and advocate for the environment. She reached out to include me on art projects. In 2008 we created a calendar with my paintings, one for each month, with her photographs of home. I have added to my letter the cover page to the calendar. Working with her was a thrill and source of pride.
> As a gift to me on my 90th birthday, she made me business cards from my paintings. I have attached on the opposite side of this page some of the cards she made for me. She was so thoughtful and generous. I loved her so much.
> It pains me that we will not ever enjoy our art together again.
> I think of Christine every day and suffer for her loss.
> Yours truly,
> Michael Sevilla

CHAPTER 9

EPILOGUE

These days, Tim Wells attends his prison's anger-management classes. He is surrounded by other men who are also incarcerated for killing their wives. They talk about their years of fights, of abuse by both parties. Tim insists to himself and other inmates that he wasn't angry toward Christine that day, or throughout their marriage. He does not recall having the feelings that other inmates describe having when they committed their crimes. He is frustrated by the classes that aim to fix a problem he does not think he has. He feels he has gotten very little out of them.

Tim argues, "If I had been angry in the conventional way, others would have picked up on it and noticed the tension. Everyone was bewildered by the murder because of this." In support of his claim, Tim recalled a prison counselor's emphatic "that's not the case!" in response to a caller on a local radio broadcast who claimed that Tim must have really hated his wife. Even when people visited him in jail, Tim wanted them to know that he didn't kill Christine out of anger. Yet when it was pointed out that strangulation is a very intimate and rage-filled way to kill another person, he could only respond, "I've read that."

How could kindly Professor Wells murder his wife by brutally strangling her and then recount the act as one of merciful love? When Tim was asked about the blunt-force injury to Christine's head, he could not reconcile it with his recollection of her loving demise. He did not know why Christine was wearing sweatpants when she was well known for dressing stylishly before going out in public. Tim insisted she had put her coat on while getting ready to leave, yet the evidentiary photographs do not show this to be the case. He rejected any possibility that a major argument erupted because Christine confronted him about not going to teach his new classes at RIT, or that she might have become so angry that she declared she wanted a divorce because of his multiple failures. To understand what appears to be delusional thinking, it is necessary to understand the phenomenon of dissociation and its power to distort reality.

In several prison interviews, Tim was questioned about the events during and after Christine's murder. Obvious gaps in his recall were apparent. With further questioning, evidence emerged that he was unable to remember critical details, particularly those that were unacceptable to his psyche. This selective forgetting suggests Tim suffered a dissociative amnesia. He is simply incapable of allowing himself to recall anything that would suggest he was capable of rage. What he remembers instead is processed through the distorted lens of his psyche, substituting an acceptable version of these events for the raw brutality of what really happened. Tim calms himself with the thought, "Yes, I murdered my wife, but it was loving and merciful."

Hours after the killing, when Tim brutishly smashed a rock onto Riley's head and saw the bloody evidence of his savagery, he was abruptly awakened from his dissociated state. The violence of his actions was undeniable. Being confronted with the horrific reality of blood spreading on Riley's head was enough to shake Tim completely from his dissociated state, returning him to his kind, intelligent, ineffectual, dependent, timid personality. He was no longer capable of brutality. Moreover, he could not go through with killing himself. With his psychological defenses utterly depleted, Tim desperately dialed 911 and cried out for help. His repressed emotions, no longer restrained, erupted in a sudden and overwhelming torrent.

Years after the murder, Tim reflected on what he hoped

people might take away from his story. "Perhaps people will puzzle over the tragedy or mourn the cruel and senseless loss. Perhaps the initial outrage and disgust will soften into wonder at how I isolated myself by hiding my fears and failures, how I neglected the need to be vulnerable, how I made it impossible for those who loved me to love me. Perhaps they will recognize the isolating loneliness that grows in loving relationships and sense the insidious burden of the well-intentioned lie. Perhaps after sharing my story, some will reclaim the joy they are missing."

In the meantime, Christine Sevilla, a passionate advocate for the environment, has not been forgotten. In August 2010, the Genesee Land Trust renamed a wetlands preserve in Caledonia, a town southwest of Rochester, in her honor. Because she had photographed and written about wetlands so often, her friends thought the most fitting memorial would

The Christine Sevilla Project continues to showcase and sell her artwork to raise money for the environment. Contact the Genesee Land Trust to inquire about purchasing her works. (Police photo)

be a wetland that was accessible to the public. They then set about raising money to build an interpretive trail, complete with informative signs, through the twenty-three-acre Christine Sevilla Wetlands Preserve and install an information kiosk. A silent auction was held on April 5, 2011, to sell Christine's many photographs. More than a hundred people purchased her works, raising a substantial amount of money for a cause very close to Christine's heart. A year later, Steven Daniel led a nature walk at the Christine Sevilla Wetlands Preserve to explore the area's birds, butterflies, dragonflies, and native plants. Her preserve also received a $180,000 gift from her estate, donated by both the Sevilla and Wells families. The inspiration that she provided for so many will live on forever.

As for Tim, time is broken into blocks meted out by prison guards. He has become a number in "a company." His routine, largely comprised of going out into the yard, eating, and attending program meetings, is dictated by lists and the barking orders of officers. Three times a day, an officer walks down Tim's cellblock while inmates call out their requests: "Twenty-three, chow"; "Twenty-two, chow and yard"; "Twenty-one, chow." Tim is number twenty. Officers strongly discourage inmates from making requests. The standard response to any inquiry is a harsh rebuke: "Didn't you hear the announcement?" and "You should have thought about that before!" Or, "You're not ready. You're not standing at your gate!"

Yard sessions and program meetings are also subject to last-minute cancelations. It is not uncommon to hear a scratchy announcement that a scheduled event has been canceled. During the winter months, groups of inmates have a gym session on Sunday evening. Gym sessions end sometime in March, replaced by an evening yard session. During the early months of his incarceration, Tim reflected, "I was hoping that this Sunday was still gym. I found myself very anxious. There was a lot of noise with inmates carrying on loud conversations cell to cell. I should have yelled out, asking if this was the day the schedule changed from gym to yard, but I couldn't bring myself to ask." He hated the idea of calling a request for gym to the guard and being rebuked. Then he realized how ridiculous it was to be anxious about the officer rejecting his request. Yet he was.

Tim found out the answer inadvertently. A prisoner called out, "Eighteen, chow and gym," only to hear the officer bark back, "No gym! Today we change to yard."

Tim was annoyed with himself for his continued inability to ask for what he needed. "For the next hour, as I waited for dinner, I wondered at my own thoughts and feelings. I was afraid to ask other inmates for clarification. I was afraid of making the wrong request. I was willing to remain in my cell rather than request information or make a mistake."

Timothy Wells is still afraid to speak up for himself. Through the long and lonely twilight of his life, he will remain in prison for a crime that might never have happened if he hadn't kept so much balled up inside. He will spend most, if not all, of the rest of his life in the Clinton Correctional penitentiary, so far away from his home at 4 Springwood Lane. Tim looked so forward to spending all his time with the fiery woman who swept into his life and stole his heart. They will take no more walks in the woods with Riley. Tim can no longer be Christine's Sherpa on her photography jaunts, a title he was so happy to have earned. All that has passed. He threw it all away.

Years after Christine's murder, Tim was asked what he would say if he could speak with Christine today. As his words reveal, he remained wistful and uncertain about the love he did or did not give to her.

Dear Christine,

Were you happy? In the years since the tragedy I am sure of less and less. I question my own memory. I know we were happy when exploring wetlands. I know we were happy when we walked Riley. I know we were happy when we sang.

I know I was happy as you grew in your artistry. I know I was happy as you worked on important causes and took meaningful stands. I know I was happy as you created your books and arts and designs. I know I was happy helping you as I could. I know I was desperate not to fail you.

I love you so much. I love our pack. I love our home and the space we created away from the world. I love the little sound you make when I tell you I'm proud of you. I worked so hard to keep you from being disappointed.

I wasn't hiding anything, was I? You and Riley are so sensitive. You knew I was hurting. You knew something was horribly wrong. You were as desperate as I was, but I didn't see it. I didn't let you in.

In my mind I was protecting you by hiding my failures, when in reality I was hurting you by not letting you help me. I believed you needed me, that you couldn't live without me, when in truth, I was being selfish and prideful by not letting you love me.

I know you would have forgiven me if I had called out to you, even after trying so hard to hide. You would have forgiven me even at that late date. Now there is a hole in the world that friends and family fill with the bewilderment and memories, questions and guesses, but in the end it cannot be filled.

After trying so hard to be a good person, I still do not know. Were you happy?

Tim

These sentiments expressed by Tim convey the sad reality that a husband and wife can be together for nearly twenty years but never really know one another. Fostering a false intimacy creates a pervasive loneliness and alienation where there should be true love. These sentiments were reflected in a haunting poem written by Christine scarcely two years before her murder:

Remembrance I

The thrush no longer comes to tell his story
His silence speaks for us
A fleeting memory of his telling, his music
    remains in our hearts
Softening the sharp ache of our loneliness

What Tim created was an upside-down world, one that was a caricature of a perfect, "wonderful" marriage (one of Tim's favorite adjectives) but in reality lacked warmth, happiness, and acceptance. This world slowly suffocated each member of the pack, even Riley. It became a zombie-like existence. People were going through the motions, occupying space and time, but devoid of fulfillment or depth. With each passing year, Tim's world unraveled further in a long, downward spiral.

Tim's overwhelming dependence, his fear of being abandoned or judged undesirable or imperfect, created a pervasive anxiety that carried him farther and farther away from his own desires and dreams. In the final months before the murder, situational stressors and multiple failures caused the wheels to fall off Tim's wagon, yet he continued his desperate struggle to hold on to the status quo. Ironically, his many secrets that he endeavored to hide from Christine were thrust into public view after her murder. In the end, the entire world came to know all of Tim's secrets that he had desperately tried to conceal.

But Tim is finally free from the paralytic mental tyranny that he felt during his marriage with Christine. The thought of this liberation rises to euphoric proportions for Tim. While he referred to that day as "the tragedy," he readily commented, "So horrible, but it felt so right." Tim will never again fear potential disappointment or disapproval from Christine. This fear is forever locked in the past. The steep cost, however, is the loss of a talented and passionate woman beloved by many and what, for Tim, seems like an eternity in prison to contemplate his actions.

Some believe that Tim's callous murder of Christine makes him a psychopath, a coldblooded killer who commits murder without remorse. But this interpretation would be wrong. Tim longs for Christine and continues to cry for her in his jail cell. The true tragedy in Tim and Christine's story is that, in Tim's genuine effort to construct the perfect marriage, the fragile world that he crafted remained vulnerable to real-life events and pernicious stressors. These events gradually eroded the tenuous basis for their shared world, until Tim no longer stood on solid ground.